The North American Third Edition

Cambridge Latin Examinations

Unit 2 Photocopiable Masters

Editor
Patricia E. Bell
Centennial Collegiate and Vocational Institute, Guelph, Ontario

Consulting Editors
Stan Farrow
David and Mary Thomson Collegiate Institute, Scarborough, Ontario

Ed Phinney
University of Massachusetts at Amherst, Amherst, Massachusetts

CAMBRIDGE
UNIVERSITY PRESS

Published by the Press Syndicate of the University of Cambridge
40 West 20th Street, New York, NY 10011-4211, USA

The Cambridge Latin Course was funded and developed by the University of Cambridge School Classics Project and SCDC Publications, London, and is published with the sponsorship of the School Curriculum Development Committee in London and the North American Cambridge Classics Project. The work of the School Curriculum Development Committee has now been taken over by the School Curriculum Assessment Authority.

First published 1995
Printed in the United States of America

ISBN 0 521 45844 7

VN

Acknowledgments

The editors wish to thank the authors of each of the Unit 2 Examinations:

Form A (1985–86) **Ed Phinney**
University of Massachusetts at Amherst, Amherst, MA

Form B (1986–87) **Elaine Batting**
Archbishop Williams High School, Braintree, MA
Carlene Craib
Westford Academy, Westford, MA

Form C (1987–88) **Elaine Batting**
Archbishop Williams High School, Braintree, MA
Carlene Craib
Westford Academy, Westford, MA

Form D (1988–89) **Stan Farrow**
David and Mary Thomson Collegiate Institute, Scarborough, Ontario

Form E (1989–90) **Elaine Batting**
Archbishop Williams High School, Braintree, MA
Carlene Craib
Westford Academy, Westford, MA

Form F (1990–91) **Patricia Freiert**
Gustavus Adolphus College, St. Peter, MN

Form G (1991–92) **Martha Beveridge**
Isidore Newman School, New Orleans, LA
Vincent Drago
St. Martin's Protestant Episcopal School, New Orleans, LA
Bee Johnson
Isidore Newman School, New Orleans, LA

Note to the teacher

This is a collection of all the examinations set annually for Unit 2 of the Cambridge Latin Course from 1985–86 to 1991–92. Each examination has an Answer Key and separate Answer Sheets.

The examinations in this collection have been edited (i.e. questions altered, expanded, or omitted) for consistency. Each examination conforms to the North American Edition of the Cambridge Latin Course and words that do not appear on the vocabulary checklists are glossed in the manner that Unit 2 words appear in the Complete Vocabulary of the student's textbook.

In each Unit 2 examination Understanding the Story has 50 points and Understanding the Background has 25 points.

The students are given **1 hour** to write each examination in Unit 2. Whenever possible, allow optimum flexibility by giving the entire examination in one sitting and allow students to answer the questions and Parts in any order they wish. If this format is not possible, give Part A: Understanding the Story in one period with a time limit of 40 minutes and Part B: Understanding the Background in another period with a time limit of 20 minutes. Distribute the Latin story in both periods, to assist with the answers.

Teachers are asked to maintain examination security i) by collecting all examination question sheets at the conclusion of the examination and ii) by ensuring that students write all their answers on the Answer Sheets that are herein provided for each examination. If desired, teachers may *temporarily* return the examination questions and graded answer sheets to the students for the purposes of discussion, but must then collect all questions and answer sheets.

Certificates of merit are available for students who obtain at least 40 points out of 50 on Part A and at least 20 points out of 25 on Part B. These certificates are available, at no charge, from the NACCP Resource Center (address below).

NACCP also continues to distribute new Cambridge Latin Examinations annually. These are available through the Resource Center of the North American Cambridge Classics Project, Box 932, Amherst, Massachusetts 01004-0932; telephone: 413–256–3564.

PART A # Understanding the story

Read the following story, and then answer the questions based on it.
Answer all questions on the Answer Sheets provided.

epistula ab Alexandrīā

Quīntus, quī in Britanniā per tōtam hiemem manēbat, epistulam ab Alexandrīā accēpit. in epistulā Clēmēns amīcus eī fābulam scrīpserat:

"heri laetissimus eram. nam hiems erat cōnfecta et diēs fēstus deae Īsidis advēnerat. ego, quod omnia vidēre volēbam, māne ad templum Augustī quam celerrimē festīnāvī. quamquam magna turba viās complēbat, locum optimum invenīre poteram. Aristō, amīcus tuus, cum suā uxōre prope mē stābat. Helena, fīlia Aristōnis, cum duōbus virīs, ūnō Graecō, alterō Aegyptiō, sermōnem habēbat.

"pompa splendida ad portum per viās veniēbat. prō pompā multae puellae, rosās ferentēs, currēbant. post multitūdinem puellārum <u>tubicinēs</u> et puerī, quī <u>carmen</u> dulce cantābant, prōcēdēbant. deinde quattuor sacerdōtēs, quī effigiem deae portābant, <u>appāruērunt</u>. nōs omnēs intentē spectābāmus.

"postquam pompa discessit, duo virī, quī cum Helenā <u>garriēbant</u>, clāmantēs pugnāre coepērunt.

"ego dē <u>salūte</u> Helenae sollicitus eram et eam ā virīs trahere temptābam. tandem Helenam servāvī, sed, ēheu, virī mē verberāre coepērunt! quamquam fortiter pugnābam, nōn <u>illīs</u> resistere poteram.

"hodiē in casā Petrōnis medicī recumbō. illī duo virī mē paene interfēcērunt. nunc necesse est mihi nihil facere. ūna rēs tamen est <u>peior</u> quam <u>iniūria</u> mea: Aristō, pater Helenae, quī pessimās <u>tragoediās</u> scrībit, saepe vīsitat et mihi <u>versūs</u> suōs recitat. ō mē miserrimum! versūs Aristōnis mē vulnerant <u>plūsquam</u> illī duo virī."

tubicen, tubicinis, m.	*trumpeter*
carmen, carminis, n.	*song*
appareō, apparēre, apparuī	*appear*
garriō, garrīre	*gossip*
salūs, salūtis, f.	*safety*
ille	*that (man)*; [*illīs* is dative plural, object of *resistere*]
peior	*worse*
iniūria, iniūriae, f.	*injury*
tragoedia, tragoediae, f.	*tragedy*
versus, versūs, m.	*verse (of a poem)*
plūsquam	*more than*

PART A Understanding the story

Answer all questions on the Answer Sheets provided.
Answer in complete English sentences (unless otherwise instructed).

1 Where was Quintus spending the winter?

2 On your Answer Sheet circle the letter of the word which correctly completes the following sentence:

Quintus received a letter from Clemens. In Quintus' father's house Clemens had once been a

A *frāter* B *lībertus* C *servus*

3 In which **country** was Clemens living at the time he wrote the letter?

4 Write one reason why Clemens was *laetissimus*.

5 Which three **Latin** words or phrases indicate that Clemens was very eager to see the festival?

6a Why was it difficult for Clemens to find a good place to watch the parade?

6b Write the **Latin** phrase which indicates whether he succeeded in finding such a place.

7 What were the nationalities of the two men with whom Helena was having a conversation?

8 On your Answer Sheet, circle the letter of the picture which shows the destination of the parade:

A

B

9 On your Answer Sheet study the picture of the parade in Alexandria. In the squares, label the following items:

Label A *puellae*
Label B *tubicinēs*
Label C *puerī*
Label D *sacerdōtēs*

10 Name in English the four groups who participated in the parade and describe the ceremonial activity of each group.

11 Which **Latin** word describes how the crowd was watching the parade?

12 After the parade passed, what **two** things did the two men do?

13a How did Clemens try to help Helena?

13b Why did Clemens do this?

13c Write the **Latin** phrase which indicates whether he succeeded.

14 Why did Clemens remark, "*ēheu*"? (line 17)

15a Where in Alexandria was Clemens on the day he was writing to Quintus?

15b What reason does he give for his being there?

16a What did Aristo do when he came there to visit Clemens?

16b Why didn't Clemens enjoy these visits?

17 What **two** superlative adjectives in the story described Clemens

i at the beginning of the day,
ii at the end of the day?

18 On your Answer Sheet, circle the letter of the word which correctly completes each of the following sentences:

i *scrīpserat* (line 2) is an example of the:
A imperfect B perfect C pluperfect

ii *clāmantēs* (line 15) is a(n):
A infinitive B imperative C participle

iii *trahere* (line 16) is a(n):
A infinitive B imperative C participle

iv *puellae* (line 10) is:
A nominative B genitive C dative

v *Helenae* (line 16) is:
A nominative B genitive C dative

19 Translate the following phrases from the story:

i *quam celerrimē festīnāvī* (line 5)
ii *nunc necesse est mihi nihil facere* (line 20)

20 Which word in the story is the **Latin** root for each of the following English words?

i advent
ii volition
iii dulcet
iv invulnerable

50 points for Part A

PART B Understanding the background

Answer all questions on the Answer Sheets provided.
Answer in complete English sentences (unless otherwise instructed).

1 On your Answer Sheet study the map which shows a route the letter-carrier may have taken from Clemens to Quintus. In the squares on your Answer Sheet label the following countries:

Label A *Ītalia*
Label B *Aegyptus*
Label C *Britannia*
Label D *Graecia*

2 Name **two** Egyptian exports which might have been loaded on the same ship carrying the letter.

3 If Quintus were to answer Clemens' letter, British exports might be loaded on the return ship carrying the letter-carrier. Name two such exports.

4 The letter from Clemens to Quintus arrived at the place pictured right. Study the picture.

4a What is the name of the modern village where this place was built?

4b What was the name of the person whom Quintus was visiting there?

4c Describe the relationship between Quintus' host and the imperial government of Rome.

4d Describe one of the administrative duties of Quintus' host.

5 Study the picture below.

5a Which harbor of Alexandria is the merchant in the picture entering?

5b What is the ancient name of the structure, partly shown at the top right of the picture?

5c Why was the structure named in 5b above one of the Seven Wonders of the Ancient World?

6 In the story of Part A, Clemens hurried to see the festival parade of the goddess Isis.

6a On your Answer Sheet circle the letter of the day of the year when the festival of Isis took place:

A September 23rd B January 1st C March 5th D June 21st

6b Why might the festival of Isis have taken place at this time of the year?

7 After Clemens was assaulted, he consulted Petro, a Greek *medicus*. Study the four pictures below.

A

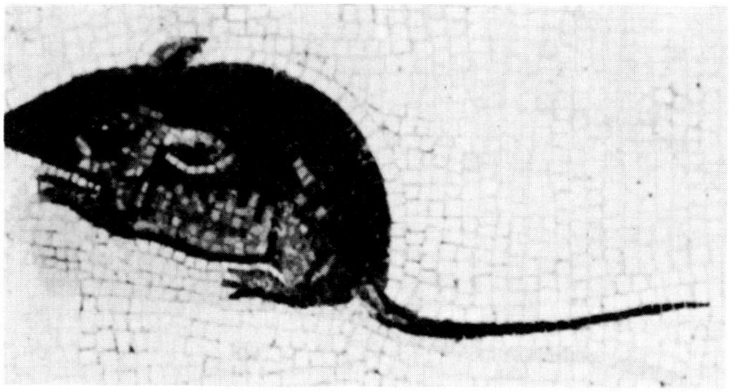

C

B

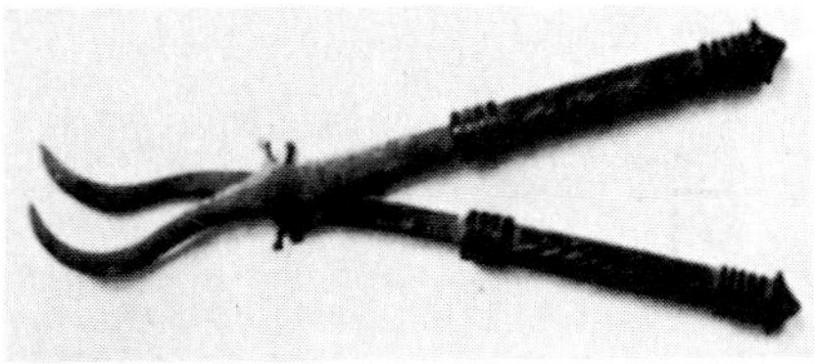

D

7a On your Answer Sheet circle the letters of two pictures which show items Petro might have used to help Clemens recover from his wounds.

7b Some practices of a first-century A.D. medical doctor were similar to the practices of a modern medical doctor. Describe three similar practices.

25 points for Part B
Total: 75 points

NOMEN ....

PART A **Understanding the story**

Answer all questions on these sheets.
Answer in complete English sentences (unless otherwise instructed).

1 ____ 1

2 A B C 1

3 ____________________ 1

4 ____ 1

5 Latin word or phrase:

i ____________________

ii ____________________

iii ____________________ 3

6a ____

____ 1

6b Latin: ____________________ 1

7 i ____________________

ii ____________________ 2

8 A B 1

9

4

10 A ______

______

______

B ______

______

______

C ______

______

______

D ______

______

______

______ ☐ 8

11 Latin: ______ ☐ 1

12 i ______

ii ______ ☐ 2

13a ______ ☐ 1

13b ______ ☐ 1

13c Latin: ______ ☐ 1

14 ______ ☐ 1

15a ______

______ ☐ 1

15b ______ ☐ 1

16a ______

______ ☐ 1

16b ______

______ ☐ 1

NOMEN ....

17 i ______________________________

ii ______________________________ ☐ 2

18 i A B C

ii A B C

iii A B C

iv A B C

v A B C ☐ 5

19 i ____ ☐ 2

ii ____ ☐ 2

20 i ______________________________

ii ______________________________

iii ______________________________

iv ______________________________ ☐ 4

/50 points for Part A

NOMEN ....

PART B **Understanding the background**

Answer all questions on these sheets.
Answer in complete English sentences (unless otherwise instructed).

1

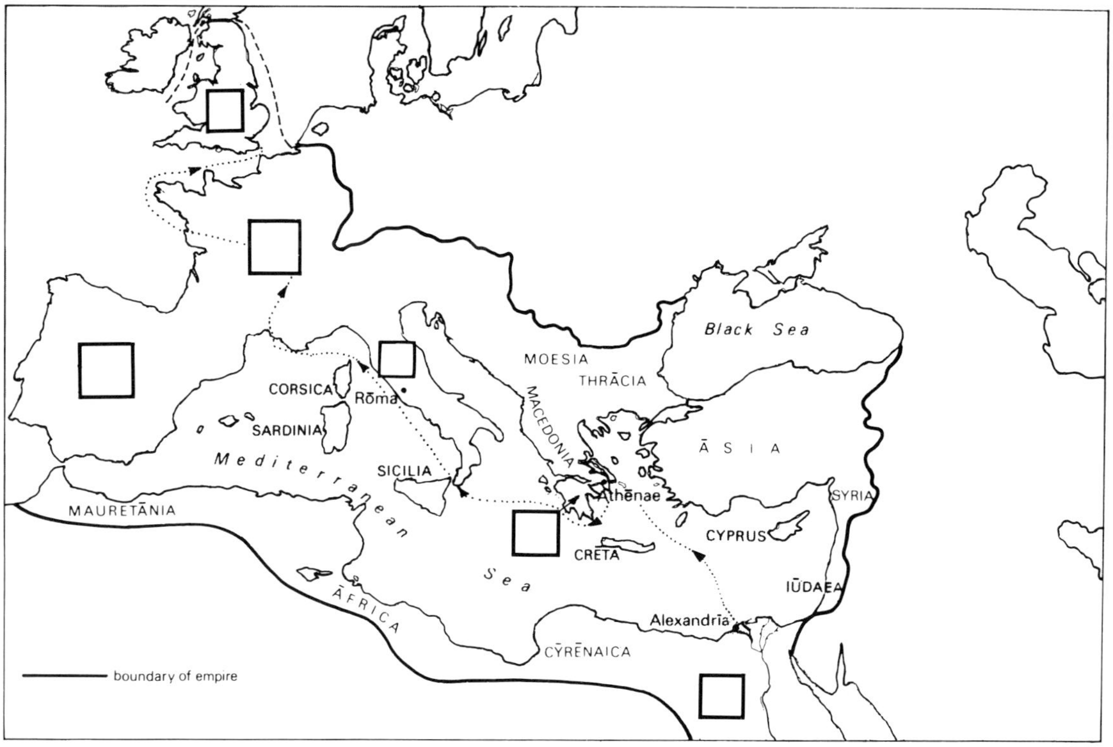

The Roman empire at the end of the first century A.D.

☐ 4

2 i ______________________

ii ______________________ ☐ 2

3 i ______________________

ii ______________________ ☐ 2

4a ______________________ ☐ 1

4b ______________________ ☐ 1

4c ______________________

____

______________________ ☐ 2

4d ____

____ ☐ 1

5a ______________________ ☐ 1

5b ______________________ ☐ 1

5c ____

____ ☐ 2

6a A B C D ☐ 1

6b ____

____ ☐ 2

7a A B C D ☐ 2

7b i ____

____

ii ____

____

iii ____

____ ☐ 3

/25 points for Part B

/50 + /25 = /75 points total

Answer Key

Each question is worth 1 point unless otherwise indicated.

PART A Understanding the story

1 Quintus was spending the winter in Britain.

2 C (*servus*)

3 Clemens was living in Egypt. (Note: the question asked for the **country**.)

4 Clemens was *laetissimus* because winter was over OR the festival/holiday of the goddess Isis had arrived.

5 any three of:
laetissimus (line 3)
(quod) omnia videre volebam (line 4)
mane (line 4)
quam celerrime (line 5)
festinavi (line 5) (3 points total)

6a It was difficult for Clemens to find a good place to watch because a great crowd filled / was filling the streets.

6b *locum optimum invenire poteram* (line 6)

7 i a Greek
ii an Egyptian (2 points total)

8 Picture A (Great Harbor)

9 Clockwise from top left: A, B, C, D; bottom squares should be left blank. (4 points)

10 The girls (1) ran ahead, carrying roses (1).
The trumpeters (1) advanced next, playing their trumpets (1).
The boys (1) advanced third, singing a sweet song (1).
Finally, four priests (1) appeared, carrying a statue of the goddess/Isis (1). (8 points total)

11 *intente* (line 13)

12 The two men started shouting and began to fight. (2 points)

13a Clemens tried to drag her away from the men.

13b Clemens tried to do this because he was worried about her safety.

13c *(tandem) Helenam servavi* (line 17)

14 Clemens remarked "*eheu*" because the men began to beat him.

15a On the day Clemens was writing to Quintus, Clemens was in the house of Petro the doctor.

15b The two men almost killed him.

16a When Aristo came to Petro's house to visit Clemens, he read his (tragic) verses to Clemens.

16b Clemens did not enjoy Aristo's visits because Aristo wrote very bad tragedies / was a very bad dramatist/poet.

17 i *laetissimus* (line 3)
ii *miserrimum* (line 22) (2 points)

18 i C (pluperfect)
ii C (participle)
iii A (infinitive)
iv A (nominative)
v B (genitive) (5 points total)

19 i "I hurried (1) as fast/quickly as possible (1)." (2 points)
ii "Now it is necessary for me (1) to do nothing (1)." (2 points)

20 i *advenerat* (line 4)
ii *volebam* (line 4)
iii *dulce* (line 11)
iv *vulnerant* (line 23)

50 points for Part A

PART B Understanding the background

1 Clockwise from left: Blank (Hispania), C, Blank (Gallia), A, D, B (4 points)

2 Any two of: wheat/corn, papyrus, glassware (2 points)

3 Any two of: grain, hunting dogs, iron (from Kent), gold (from Wales), tin (from Cornwall), lead (from Derbyshire and Clwyd) (2 points)

4a Fishbourne

4b Cogidubnus / King of the Regnenses

4c Any two points: After the Roman invasion in A.D. 43, the Romans appointed Cogidubnus king of the Atrebates/Regnenses tribespeople. The appointment may have been his reward for helping the Emperor Claudius at the time of the invasion. King Cogidubnus was a strong supporter of the Roman power. Cogidubnus became a "client king." (2 points)

4d Any one of: Cogidubnus ruled the Regnenses on behalf of the emperor. He collected taxes for the Romans from the Regnenses. He kept the peace in his part of Britain. He kept the southern part of Britain loyal to Rome, while Agricola and the Roman legions conquered the west and north.

5a Great Harbor (of Alexandria)

5b Pharos

5c Any two details: The Pharos was very high (122 meters / 400 feet), and a fire was always burning at the top to guide the thousands of ships that entered the Great Harbor. (2 points)

6a C (March 5th)

6b Any two details: Just as Isis had helped her husband Osiris resurrect, so she was thought to be responsible for the new life at springtime (which in Egypt appeared after the annual flooding of the Nile). The March 5th festival was held at the beginning of spring, when the sailing season opened. (2 points)

7a B (*forfex*: "scissors") and D (spiderweb) (2 points)

7b Any three of:
Both Roman-period and modern doctors might treat some ailments with drugs.
Both doctors might practice some surgery.
Both doctors might make incisions to tie veins and arteries.
Both doctors might reset broken bones with splints.
Both doctors might stitch up wounds.
Both doctors might amputate a limb.
Both doctors might insist on hygiene to reduce risk of infection. (3 points total)

25 points for Part B

Total: 75 points

PART A Understanding the story

Read the following story, and then answer the questions based on it.
Answer all questions on the Answer Sheets provided.

somnium Euporis

Eupor, quī erat medicus Graecus, in urbe Athēnīs habitābat. ōlim, postquam cēnam cōnsūmpsit, in hortō ambulābat, et dē Rūfō, amīcō Alexandrīnō, cōgitābat. deinde Eupor cubiculum intrāvit fessus et obdormīvit. mox somniāre coepit.

in somniō flūmen Nīlum, in quō multī crocodīlī hippopotamīque natābant, vīdit. subitō servum clāmantem audīvit. "servā Barbillum!" exclāmābat servus, "servā Barbillum! hippopotamus eum in aquam dēiēcit, et nunc Barbillus in maximō perīculō est!"

cubiculum quoque, ubi Barbillus in lectō recumbēbat, vīdit. Petrō, quī magister amīcusque Euporis in urbe Alexandrīā fuerat, prope lectum stābat.

"ego dē vītā eius dēspērō," inquit Petrō, "quod medicāmentum astrologī est pessimum et vulnus ingravēscit."

dēnique Barbillus in aurem Petrōnis susurrāvit, "moritūrus sum. veniam ā Rūfō petere volō quod eī magnam iniūriam intulī."

Eupor statim ē lectō surrēxit et uxōrem excitāvit. "necesse est mihi," inquit, "Rūfum invenīre."

"cūr necesse est tibi Rūfum invenīre?" rogāvit uxor.

"post mortem Plōtīnae Barbillus Rūfum diū vituperāre solēbat," respondit Eupor, "sed Barbillus, ubi periit, veniam Rūfō absentī dedit. ō Rūfe miserrime, ubi es?"

"quō modō haec omnia cognōvistī?" rogāvit uxor.

"in somniō meō Barbillum vulnerātum vīdī et audīvī," respondit marītus.

"num somniō tuō crēdis? tū es medicus doctus et nōtus, nōn astrologus superstitiōsus!"

Eupor, quamquam uxōrī maximē cōnfīdēbat, nōn eī cessit. "perīculōsum est nōbīs," inquit Eupor, "hoc somnium dērīdēre. ego dē naufrāgiō, in quō posteā māter Rūfī periit, ōlim somniāvī sed nihil fēcī. nunc igitur necesse est mihi Rūfum quaerere et dē veniā patris eī nārrāre."

uxor, valdē commōta, marītō dīxit, "Eupor cārissime, nōlī diūtius domī manēre. decōrum est tibi, amīcō fidēlī, amīcum miserum statim adiuvāre. ī nunc, sed ad mē quam celerrimē redī."

somnium, somniī, n.	*dream*
somniō, somniāre, somniāvī	*dream*
natō, natāre	*swim*
dēiciō, dēicere, dēiēcī	*throw down*
fuerat	*had been*
medicāmentum, medicāmentī, n.	*medication*
ingravēscit	*grows worse*
venia, veniae, f.	*mercy, forgiveness*
iniūria, iniūriae, f.	*injustice, injury*
quō modō?	*how?*
haec omnia	*all these things*
cōnfīdō, cōnfīdere	*trust*
cēdō, cēdere, cessī	*give in, yield*
naufrāgium, naufrāgiī, n.	*shipwreck*
diūtius	*any longer*
domī	*at home*
adiuvō, adiuvāre	*help*
ī (from īre)	*go!*

PART A Understanding the story

Answer all questions on the Answer Sheets provided.
Answer in complete English sentences (unless otherwise instructed).

1 On your Answer Sheet, circle the correct letter. Eupor was a:

A soothsayer B doctor C teacher

2 At what time of the day did the story take place?

3 State **five** things Eupor did in the first paragraph.

4 On your Answer Sheet, circle the letter of the picture which shows what Eupor first saw in his dream:

A

B

5 Write the **Latin** word in line 6 which tells what Eupor heard the slave doing, then translate it.

6 On your Answer Sheet, circle the letters which give the two scenes in Eupor's dream (lines 5–9):

A garden B dining-room C river D study E bedroom

7 Write the two **Latin** words in line 10 which describe Petro's relationship with Eupor.

8a Where was Petro in Eupor's dream?

8b State two reasons why Petro in the dream said he despaired for Barbillus' life.

9 Write the **Latin** word in line 16 which tells you **when** Eupor woke his wife. Then translate it.

10a What was it that we may deduce (from lines 19–20) that **Rufus** did not know?

10b How did Eupor find out what Rufus did not know? (lines 22–24)

10c According to line 21, what did **Eupor** not know?

11a Why was Eupor's wife surprised he believed his dream? (lines 25–26)

11b What reason did Eupor give for believing this dream? (lines 28–29)

12 Why do you think Eupor's wife was *valdē commōta*? (line 32)

13 What two things in line 34 did Eupor's wife tell him to do?

14 Circle the letter which gives the best way to translate *susurrāvit* (line 14):

A hesitated B whispered C sobbed

15 Translate the following:

i *post mortem Plōtīnae Barbillus Rūfum diū vituperāre solēbat.* (line 19)
ii *num somniō tuō crēdis?* (line 25)

16 Write the command (two words) which appears in line 6, and then translate it.

17 In lines 16–17 what was it necessary for Eupor to do? Write the two **Latin** words, and then translate them.

18 Write the superlative adjective which describes Rufus in line 21. Then translate it.

19 From the story find one example of each of the following:

i a noun in the dative case
ii a noun in the genitive case
iii a verb in the imperfect tense
iv a verb in the perfect tense

20 Circle the correct answer: *cārissime*, the adjective in line 32, is:

A nominative case B dative case C vocative case

21 From the story find the **Latin** word which is the root for each of the following English derivatives:

i cogitate
ii perilous
iii vitality
iv derision

50 points for Part A

PART B Understanding the background

Answer all questions on the Answer Sheets provided.
Answer in complete English sentences (unless otherwise instructed).

1 Study the map of the Roman empire on your Answer Sheet. Label the map with the appropriate letter for each place where each of the following events from Unit 2 occurred:

Label A: *hippopotamus Barbillum in aquam dēiēcit.*
Label B: *Eupor artem medicīnae exercēbat.*
Label C: *Rūfus in exercitū Rōmānō mīlitāvit.*

2 Write one reason why Eupor would have chosen to study medicine in Alexandria.

3 Name two architecturally outstanding structures which Eupor might have seen when he was a student in Alexandria, and then describe each of the two with one sentence.

4 Study the picture on the right. Answer the following questions based on the picture:

i Which craft, for which Alexandria was famous, is being practiced?
ii What is the workman in the background doing?
iii What is the workman in the foreground doing?
iv What is the boy, who is squatting in the center, doing?

5 Besides the Greeks, name two other nationalities which had substantial populations in Alexandria.

6 Why were the Greeks the most powerful and influential of these nationalities in Alexandria?

7 Study the three pictures (which illustrate the annual procession of Isis in Alexandria) on your Answer Sheets. Label each with the appropriate letter:

Label A: *pompa ad templum Serāpidis advenit.*
Label B: *puellae corōnās rosārum geruns et rosās spargunt.*
Label C: *quattuor sacerdōtēs statuam Īsidis portant.*

8 Describe, with a sentence or two, the other two main events of the festival of Isis, which took place in Alexandria every March 5th:

i Ceremony at the Great Harbor.
ii Return of Isis to the Temple of Serapis.

9 Eupor, if he reached Britain on his quest to find Rufus, might have sought information from Salvius about Rufus' whereabouts. Why would Salvius have had information about the various legions' locations?

10 Who was the Roman governor of Britain when Eupor might have visited there (A.D. 82)?

11 Which Roman emperor succeeded, in A.D. 43, in invading Britain and making it a province of the Roman empire?

25 points for Part B
Total: 75 points

NOMEN ....

PART A

Understanding the story

Answer all questions on these sheets.
Answer in complete English sentences (unless otherwise instructed).

1 A B C ☐ 1

2 ______________________________ ☐ 1

3 ______________________________

____

____

____

____

______________________________ ☐ 5

4 A B ☐ 1

5 Latin: ______________________________

Translation: ______________________________ ☐ 2

6 A B C D E ☐ 2

7 i ______________________________

ii ______________________________ ☐ 2

8a ______________________________ ☐ 1

8b i ______________________________

ii ______________________________ ☐ 2

9 Latin: ______________________________

Translation: ______________________________ ☐ 2

10a ______________________________

______________________________ ☐ 1

10b ______________________________

______________________________ ☐ 1

10c ____

____ ☐ 1

11a ____ ☐ 1

11b ____

____ ☐ 2

12 ____

____

____ ☐ 1

13 ____

____ ☐ 2

14 A B C ☐ 1

15 i ____

____ ☐ 4

ii ____

____ ☐ 2

16 Latin: ____________________

Translation: ____________________ ☐ 2

17 Latin: ____________________

Translation: ____________________ ☐ 2

18 Latin: ____________________

Translation: ____________________ ☐ 2

19 i ____________________ ii ____________________

iii ____________________ iv ____________________ ☐ 4

20 A B C ☐ 1

21 i ____________________ ii ____________________

iii ____________________ iv ____________________ ☐ 4

/50 points for Part A

NOMEN ....

PART B Understanding the background

Answer all questions on these sheets.
Answer in complete English sentences (unless otherwise instructed).

1

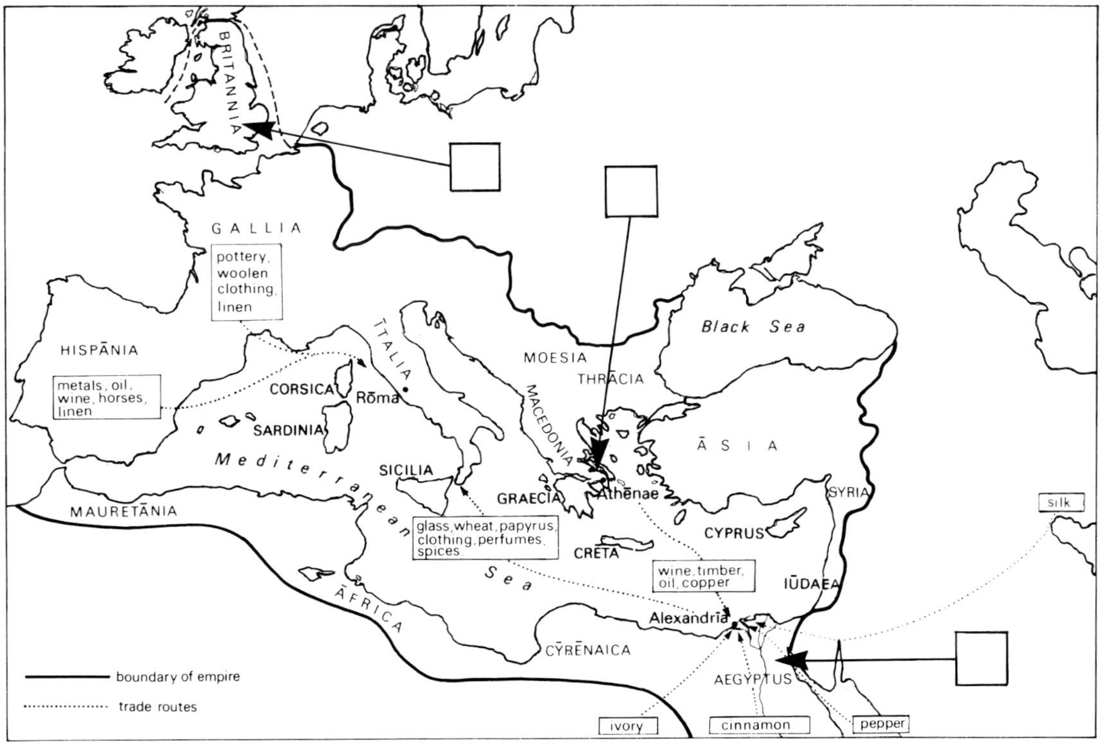

The Roman empire at the end of the first century A.D.

☐ 3

2 ______________________________

______________________________ ☐ 1

3 i Name: ______________________________

Description: ______________________________

____

ii Name: ______________________________

Description: ______________________________

______________________________ ☐ 4

4 i ______________________________

ii ______________________________

____

iii ______________________________

____

iv ______________________________

______________________________ ☐ 4

5 i ______________________________

ii ______________________________ ☐ 2

6 ______________________________

____

______________________________ ☐ 1

7

☐ 3

NOMEN ....

8 i ______________________________

____

____

ii ______________________________

____

______________________________ ☐ 4

9 ______________________________

______________________________ ☐ 1

10 ______________________________ ☐ 1

11 ______________________________ ☐ 1

/25 points for Part B

/50 + /25 = /75 points total

Answer Key

Each question is worth 1 point unless otherwise indicated.

PART A Understanding the story

1 B (doctor)

2 The story took place after dinner (at night).

3 Eupor went for a walk in the garden, and thought about Rufus. (Then) he entered his bedroom, fell asleep, and began to dream. (5 points—1 point for each item.)

4 Picture B

5 *clamantem*: "shouting" (2 points)

6 C (river) and E (bedroom) (2 points)

7 i *magister* ii *amicus* (2 points)

8a He was standing near the bed (where Barbillus was lying).

8b i The astrologer's medication is very bad.
ii The wound is growing worse. (2 points total)

9 *statim*: "at once" (after getting up) (2 points)

10a We may deduce that Rufus did not know his father Barbillus had forgiven him on his death bed.

10b Eupor saw and heard the wounded Barbillus in his dream.

10c Eupor did not know where Rufus was.

11a Eupor's wife was surprised he believed his dream because he was educated (he was a doctor, not a superstitious astrologer).

11b He once dreamed about the shipwreck in which afterwards Rufus' mother died, but did nothing (to warn them ahead of time). OR He had once ignored a dream involving Rufus' family which afterwards turned out to be true. (2 points)

12 There are several possibilities why Eupor's wife was "very alarmed": She was persuaded that her husband's frightening dream about Barbillus' death bed was true and therefore had to be acted upon. She realized that she would have to let her husband go in search of Rufus, and she would miss him. She was afraid that if Eupor went in search of Rufus, he might get hurt or even killed.

13 Eupor's wife told him to go and return (as quickly as possible). (2 points)

14 B (whispered)

15 i After Plotina's death (1), Barbillus for a long time (1) was accustomed to cursing / finding fault with Rufus (2). (4 points total)
ii (Surely) you don't believe your dream, do you? (2 points total)

16 *serva Barbillum!*: "Save Barbillus!" (2 points)

17 *Rufum invenire*: "to find Rufus" (2 points)

18 *miserrime*: "very sad" (2 points)

19 i *Rufo* (line 20), *somnio* (line 25), *uxori* (line 27), *marito* (line 32), *amico* (line 33)
ii *Euporis* (line 10), *astrologi* (line 13), *Petronis* (line 14), *Plotinae* (line 19), *patris* (line 30)
iii many examples
iv many examples

20 C (vocative)

21 i *cogitabat* (line 3)
ii *periculo* (line 8), *periculosum* (line 28)
iii *vita* (line 12) iv *deridere* (line 28)

50 points for Part A

PART B Understanding the background

1 Label A: Egypt (Aegyptus)
Label B: Athens (Athenae)
Label C: Britain (Britannia) (3 points total)

2 Any one item: Several centuries earlier than Eupor, the Greek rulers of Egypt invited to Alexandria intelligent men, among them doctors continuing the medical traditions of Hippocrates. But in Alexandria medicine rapidly developed as a science because of the advances in the knowledge of human anatomy which resulted from the dissection of corpses, an Egyptian practice of long-standing. Herophilus was the most famous Alexandrian anatomist.

3 Any two items (4 points total):
The Pharos. The Pharos was a huge lighthouse which stood on a little island just outside the Great Harbor.
The Caesareum. The Caesareum was a temple which had been begun by Cleopatra in honor of Marc Antony, but had been completed by the Emperor Augustus in honor of himself.
The Museum. The Museum was essentially a university, with a library containing more than half a million volumes.
Other possibilities are the two obelisks in front of the Caesareum (one now on the Thames, the other in New York City's Central Park), the Royal Quarters, or the Serapeum (Temple of Serapis and Isis).

4 i The picture illustrates the craft of glass-blowing.
ii The workman in the background is lifting a blob of molten glass out of an ore furnace.
iii The workman in the foreground is blowing down a pipe into a blob of molten glass attached to the end of the pipe.
iv The boy is increasing the draft to the furnace-fire with a bellows. (4 points total)

5 The major possibilities are: (Native) Egyptians, Jews, Romans, Africans, Indians. (2 points)

6 The Greeks had planned and built the city which Alexander the Great founded, and they still ran it during the Roman occupation. Theirs was the official language, and many of them were wealthy and enjoyed political privileges.

7 Label A: Picture at bottom
Label B: Picture at top left
Label C: Picture at top right (3 points)

8 i Any two details: At the harbor, the high priest dedicated a ritual ship to Isis. The priests and people loaded it with spices and flowers, and finally launched it. (2 points)
ii Any two details: The statue of Isis was carried back to the Temple of Serapis, where it was replaced. A priest on a raised platform read to the people from a holy book, and prayed for the Roman people, their emperor, and the safety of their ships and sailors. (2 points)

9 Salvius had been posted to Britain as a law commissioner of the Roman government, and would have traveled widely over the province while performing his duties.

10 Agricola

11 Claudius

25 points for Part B
Total: 75 points

PART A

Understanding the story

Read the following story, and then answer the questions based on it. Answer all questions on the Answer Sheets provided.

memoriae Pompēiānae

Quīntus et Clēmēns, postquam ad urbem Athēnās advēnērunt, per viās urbis ambulābant. sermōnem inter sē habēbant. Clēmentem, quī iam lībertus erat, Quīntus dē cōnsiliīs eius rogābat. volēbat enim Clēmentem adiuvāre.

"quid vīs," rogāvit Quīntus, "nunc facere? vīsne in Graeciā manēre?"

"minimē," respondit Clēmēns. "ad urbem Alexandrīam, quae domus deae Īsidis est, īre volō. locum unde prīmō Īsis vēnit vidēre valdē cupiō. nam Īsis mē servāvit, ubi iste Vesuvius urbem Pompēiōs dēlēvit."

"ex urbe Athēnīs ad urbem Alexandrīam iter facere vīs?" rogāvit Quīntus. "facile est nōbīs hoc facere, quod multam pecūniam habeō."

"ita vērō, domine," respondit Clēmēns. "ibi tabernam emere velim. nam tabernam tenēre diu volō. sed vērē mēcum venīre vīs?"

"certē tēcum ad Aegyptum īre volō!" exclāmāvit Quīntus. "in illā terrā sunt multae rēs, quās vidēre cupiō. exemplī grātiā, sunt in Aegyptō multae pȳramides, quās Aegyptiī ōlim exstrūxērunt. Aegyptiī in pȳramidibus rēgēs sepelīre solēbant. ego pȳramidas vidēre volō quod sunt maximae et pulcherrimae. praetereā, ad Ītaliam redīre nōlō."

in viā, ubi Quīntus Clēmēnsque ambulābant, nōnnūllī puerī Graecī discum ēmittēbant. Quīntus, eōs spectāns, Clēmentī dīxit,

"cum patre meō ōlim ad palaestram Pompēiōrum adiī. discum novum habuī, quod diem nātālem celebrābam. āthlēta nōtissimus erat in palaestrā. discum meum ēmīsī, et ita nāsum statuae, quae in palaestrā stābat, frēgī. āthlēta īrātissimus erat, quod statua sē simulābat."

postquam Quīntus hanc rem nārrāvit, quīdam puer ad eum cucurrit et eī discum obtulit. Quīntus discum accēpit, et eum ēmittere coepit. deinde statuam pulcherrimam deae Athēnae prope viam cōnspēxit. discum puerō statim reddidit.

"tū discum ēmitte, *παιδίον μου*," inquit rīdēns. "ego aliam statuam frangere nōlō!"

Clēmēns, quī Quīntum puerumque spectābat, quoque rīdēbat, sed puer Graecus verba Latīna nōn intellēxerat. ad suōs amīcōs Graecōs statim rediit.

Quīntus et Clēmēns prōcēdēbant. Quīntus, dē diē nātālī illō parentibusque suīs cōgitāns, trīstissimus erat. suspīrāvit et, "ad urbem Pompēiōs," inquit, "redīre nōn possum."

memoria, memoriae, f.	*memory*
Athēnae	*Athens*
adiuvō, adiuvāre	*help*
Graecia, Graeciae, f.	*Greece*
unde	*from where*
prīmō	*first*
velim	*I would like*
vērē	*really*
certē	*certainly*
Aegyptus, Aegyptī, f.	*Egypt*
exemplī grātiā	*for example*
pȳramis, pȳramidis, f.	*pyramid*
exstruō, exstruere, exstrūxī	*build*
sepeliō, sepelīre	*bury*
praetereā	*besides*
nōnnūllī	*several*
palaestra, palaestrae, f.	*palaestra, exercise ground*
nāsus, nāsī, m.	*nose*
sē simulābat	*represented him*
quīdam	*a certain*
Athēna, Athēnae	*the goddess Athena, patroness of Athens*
παιδίον μου = paidion mu	*my little child (in the Greek language)*
verbum, verbī, n.	*word*
suspīrō, suspīrāre, suspīrāvī	*sigh*

PART A Understanding the story

Answer all questions on the Answer Sheets provided.
Answer in complete English sentences (unless otherwise instructed).

1a What **two** things were Quintus and Clemens doing, after they had arrived in Athens? (lines 1–2)

1b What case is *urbis*? (line 2)

1c Why did Quintus ask Clemens about his plans?

2 Identify two infinitives in lines 5–6, and write them in Latin.

3a Where did Clemens want to go? (lines 7–8)

3b What was special about this place? (lines 7–8)

3c What had the goddess Isis done for Clemens? (lines 9–10)

4 What did Quintus think of Clemens' idea? (line 12)

5a In line 12, find a noun–adjective pair, write it in Latin, and translate it.

5b What case are the noun and adjective in this pair?

5c What gender are they—masculine or feminine?

6 What did Clemens want to do in Alexandria? (line 13)

7a Translate the sentence:

in illā terrā sunt multae rēs, quās vidēre cupiō. (lines 15–16)

7b On your Answer Sheet, underline the relative clause in this Latin sentence.

7c Circle the relative pronoun.

7d Put a box around the noun in the main clause to which the relative pronoun refers.

8a What did Quintus want to see in Egypt? (line 18)

8b For what purpose had the Egyptians built these structures? (lines 17–18)

9 Why do you think Quintus did not want to return to Italy? (line 19)

10 What were the Greek boys doing in the street? (lines 20–21)

11 Find a present participle in line 21, write it in Latin, and then translate it into English.

12 Briefly outline the incident which Quintus remembered because of the boys' activity. (lines 22–26)

13a What accident happened during this incident?

13b What case is *statuae*? (line 24)

14a Who was *īrātissimus?* (line 25)

14b Why was this person *īrātissimus?*

15 What happened first after Quintus had finished telling the story? (lines 27–28)

16a What did Quintus begin to do with the discus? (line 28)

16b What stopped him from finishing? (line 29)

16c What did he finally do with the discus? (line 30)

17 Translate the command, *tū discum ēmitte.* (line 31)

18 Explain the connection between Quintus' comment in lines 31–32, *ego aliam statuam frangere nōlō!* and his reminiscence in lines 22–26.

19 What was one thing Clemens was doing while this scene (lines 27–32) was taking place? (line 33)

20 What tense is *intellēxerat?* (line 34)

21 What did the Greek boy do after Quintus had spoken to him? (lines 34–35)

22a Write the Latin word in line 37 that describes how Quintus was feeling, and give its meaning.

22b Why was he feeling this way?

23 Translate line 38 (the last sentence of the story).

24 From the story, find the root for each of the following English words:

i deleterious
ii infringe
iii volition

50 points for Part A

PART B Understanding the background

Answer all questions on the Answer Sheets provided.
Answer in complete English sentences (unless otherwise instructed).

1 Refer to the map below to complete the following statements about Quintus' travels after the destruction of Pompeii. On your Answer Sheet circle the letter which correctly completes each statement.

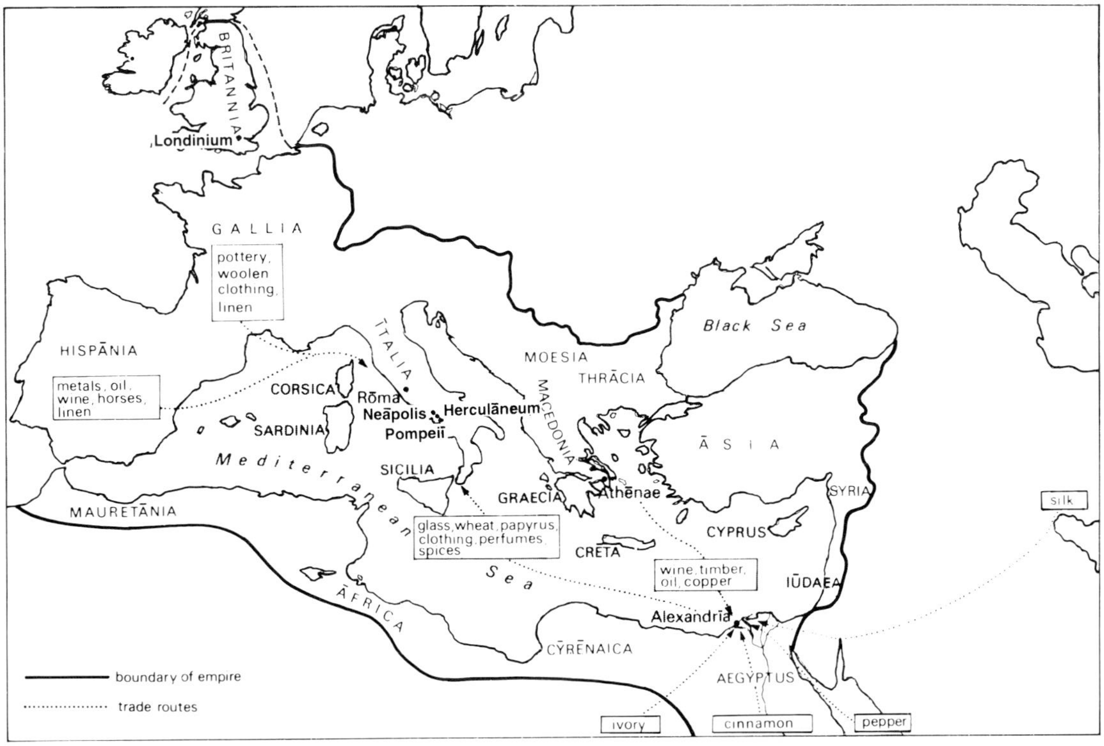

The Roman empire at the end of the first century A.D.

1a *postquam Vesuvius urbem Pompēiōs dēlēvit, Quīntus ad urbem* __________ *effūgit.*

A *Rōmam* B *Neāpolim* C *Herculāneum*

1b *deinde, Quīntus et Clēmēns ad* __________ *nāvigāvērunt.*

A *Britanniam* B *Aegyptum* C *Graeciam*

1c *ab urbe Athēnīs, ad urbem* __________ *iter fēcērunt.*

A *Alexandrīam* B *Londinium* C *Rōmam*

1d *Quīntus tandem ad* __________ *advēnit.*

A *Ītaliam* B *Graeciam* C *Britanniam*

2 In lines 15–19 of the story, Quintus talks about the attractions Egypt holds for him. Name two points of interest in Alexandria itself (e.g., famous landmarks or pieces of architecture) that might attract Quintus to the city.

3 Clemens discusses the goddess Isis in lines 7–10. On your Answer Sheet circle the letter which describes Isis. Isis was mainly a goddess of:

A life and rebirth B death and burial C medicine and healing

4 Isis was married to:

A Ptolemy B Serapis C Osiris

5a At what time of the year was the festival of Isis celebrated?

5b Give one reason for this.

6 The god pictured right, who was thought to be responsible for crops and the harvest, was called:

A Plancus
B Horus
C Serapis

7 Give two reasons why Alexandria became a major commercial center of the ancient world.

8 Give one reason why Alexandria was an important center for study and research.

9 Alexandria was also famous for the glassware sold there. What technique, discovered in the late first century B.C. and still practiced by modern craftsmen, revolutionized the glassmaking industry?

10 "Millefiori" was a type of decoration in which:

A molten glass was wrapped around a core of sand or clay which was later scraped out.
B small pieces of colored glass were arranged in a pattern around a mold.
C glass was chemically colored by trailing thin lines of molten glass onto a finished vessel.

11 In his travels, Quintus visited both Britain and Egypt. Describe how his experience of Alexandria would have differed from his experience of Britain in each of the following respects:

i climate
ii the advance of civilization

12 In Roman Britain, the supremacy of the Roman conquerors was uncontested, except occasionally by the Britons themselves. In Roman Egypt, and particularly Alexandria, this was not the case; that is, the Romans were not the only powerful foreign group. Explain this circumstance, with reference to each of the following questions:

12a Who was the founder of Alexandria?

12b Which nation therefore rightly took the credit for the planning and construction of the city?

12c What kind of incidents among the native population resulted from the occupation of the city by two powerful groups simultaneously? (Consider the story of Quintus and his Egyptian slave-boy.)

13a What was one policy the Romans used in **Britain** in an attempt to keep control there?

13b This inscription was found in the town of Chichester in England.

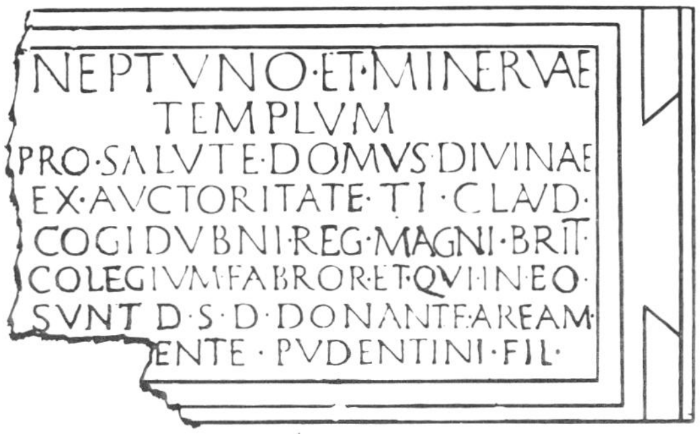

Find three clues from this inscription which help show that the Romans were indeed taking control, at least over some Britons.

25 points for Part B
Total: 75 points

NOMEN ....

PART A Understanding the story

Answer all questions on these sheets.
Answer in complete English sentences (unless otherwise instructed).

1a ______________________________
______________________________ ☐ 2

1b ______________ ☐ 1

1c ______________________________
______________________________ ☐ 1

2 Latin: ______________
Latin: ______________ ☐ 2

3a ______________ ☐ 1

3b ______________________________
______________________________ ☐ 1

3c ______________________________
______________________________ ☐ 1

4 ______________________________
______________________________ ☐ 1

5a Latin: ______________
Translation: ______________ ☐ 2

5b ______________ ☐ 1

5c ______________ ☐ 1

6 ______________________________ ☐ 1

7a ______________________________
______________________________ ☐ 2

NOMEN ....

7b,c,d *in illa terra sunt multae res, quas videre cupio.* [ ] 3

8a ______ [ ] 1

8b ______ [ ] 1

9 ______ [ ] 1

10 ______ [ ] 1

11 Latin: ______
Translation: ______ [ ] 2

12 ______ [ ] 2

13a ______ [ ] 1

13b ______ ______ [ ] 1

14a ______ [ ] 1

14b ______ [ ] 1

15 ______ [ ] 1

16a ______ [ ] 1

16b ______ [ ] 1

16c ______ [ ] 1

NOMEN ....

17 ____ ☐ 1

18 ____

____

____

____ ☐ 2

19 ____ ☐ 1

20 ______________________ ☐ 1

21 ____

____ ☐ 1

22a Latin: ______________________

Translation: ______________________ ☐ 2

22b ____

____ ☐ 1

23 ____

____ ☐ 2

24 i ______________________

ii ______________________

iii ______________________ ☐ 3

/50 points for Part A

NOMEN ....

PART B **Understanding the background**

Answer all questions on these sheets.
Answer in complete English sentences (unless otherwise instructed).

1a A B C □ 1

1b A B C □ 1

1c A B C □ 1

1d A B C □ 1

2 i ____________________

ii ____________________ □ 2

3 A B C □ 1

4 A B C □ 1

5a ____ □ 1

5b ____

____ □ 1

6 A B C □ 1

7 ____

____

____ □ 2

8 ____

____ □ 1

9 ____ □ 1

10 A B C □ 1

NOMEN ....

11 i ____________________

____

ii ____________________

____________________ ☐ 2

12a ____________________ ☐ 1

12b ____________________ ☐ 1

12c ____________________

____

____________________ ☐ 1

13a ____________________ ☐ 1

13b ____________________

____

____

____________________ ☐ 3

/25 points for Part B

/50 + /25 = /75 points total

Answer Key

Each question is worth 1 point unless otherwise indicated.

PART A Understanding the story

1a Quintus and Clemens were walking through the city streets having a conversation. (2 points)

1b *urbis* is in the genitive case.

1c Quintus was asking Clemens about his plans because he wanted to help Clemens.

2 *facere, manere* (2 points)

3a Clemens wanted to go to the city of Alexandria.

3b Alexandria was the home of the goddess Isis.

3c Isis had saved Clemens when (the eruption of) Mount Vesuvius destroyed Pompeii.

4 Quintus thought it would be easy to carry out Clemens' suggestion (because he (Quintus) had a lot of money).

5a *multam pecuniam*: much money (2 points)

5b the accusative case

5c feminine

6 Clemens wanted to buy a shop in Alexandria.

7a In that land there are many things (1) which I want to see (1). (2 points total)

7b,c,d *in illa terra sunt multae* [*res*], (*quas*) *<u>videre cupio</u>*. (3 points)

8a Quintus wanted to see the pyramids in Egypt.

8b The Egyptians had built the pyramids in order to bury their kings in them.

9 Answers may vary, but in the story "Quintus de se," Unit 2, page 68, Quintus remarks "*tum ex Italia discedere volui, quod tristissimus eram*" (lines 10–11): "Then I wanted to leave Italy, because I was very sad." Presumably his reason for not wanting to go back to Italy from Greece is the same: memories of the tragedy at Pompeii are still too recent and painful.

10 They were throwing the discus.

11 *spectans*: watching (2 points)

12 Any two details: Quintus was remembering his birthday visit with his father to the palaestra in Pompeii where he got to throw his discus (his birthday present). (2 points)

13a Quintus broke a statue's nose in this incident.

13b *statuae* is in the genitive case.

14a An athlete was *iratissimus* (very angry).

14b The statue whose nose got broken was a statue of him.

15 One of the boys ran up to Quintus and offered him a discus.

16a Quintus began to throw the discus.

16b He caught sight of a very beautiful statue of Athena near the street.

16c He gave the discus back to the boy.

17 "You throw the discus."

18 Any two details: Quintus does not throw the discus that the boy has handed him, because he has noticed a beautiful statue of Athena nearby. He says to the boy, "I don't want to break another statue," because he has just remembered breaking the nose of the athlete's statue in the palaestra at Pompeii the day (his birthday) when he and his father visited the palaestra and he struck the statue with his discus when he threw it. (2 points)

19 One detail: Clemens was watching Quintus and the boy and he was laughing.

20 pluperfect tense

21 The Greek boy immediately went back to his Greek friends after Quintus spoke to him.

22a *tristissimus*: very sad (2 points)

22b He was remembering his parents and/or his birthday.

23 "I cannot go back (1) to the city of Pompeii," he said (1). (2 points total)

24 i *delevit* (line 10)
ii *fregi* (line 25); *frangere* (line 32)
iii various forms of *volo* throughout the story (3 points total)

50 points for Part A

PART B Understanding the background

1a B (*Neapolim*)

1b C (*Graeciam*)

1c A (*Alexandriam*)

1d C (*Britanniam*)

2 Answers will vary, but may include that Quintus might have wanted to see the Pharos lighthouse, the harbors of Alexandria, the Caesareum, the Serapeum, the Museum with its library, Cleopatra's Needles, etc. (2 points)

3 A (life and rebirth)

4 C (Osiris)

5a The festival of Isis was celebrated on March 5th (end of winter / beginning of spring) annually.

5b Answers may vary, but should suggest that, as Isis was a goddess associated with the renewal of life, the springtime was a fitting time to hold a festival in her honor, when the growth of crops followed the flooding of the Nile; the fact that this was also the opening of the sailing season might also be mentioned, since part of the festival of Isis involved launching a ceremonial ship in her honor.

6 C (Serapis)

7 Any two points: Alexandria was ideally situated on the north coast of Africa, where it was accessible by sea to many parts of the ancient world. It was also well supplied with natural resources, such as fresh water from the Nile (and the freshwater lake behind the city, connected by canals to the Nile), and limestone. There was also a good natural harbor. When Alexander selected the site as a place to found a city, he committed the task to an architect who made use of the city's advantages, and the result was a well-planned city of Greek design with three excellent harbors: the natural harbor was divided into two by the construction of a breakwater, and the freshwater lake served as a third harbor. All of these factors contributed to the development of Alexandria as an important commercial center in the ancient world. (2 points)

8 Any one point: Alexandria was an important center for study and research primarily because of the great Museum and library, which had been established there by Greek rulers of Egypt, and attracted scholars in many disciplines (such as medicine and the other sciences), from all over the Greek world, who made great advancements in their fields in the course of their work at Alexandria.

9 The discovery of the technique of glass-blowing revolutionized the glassmaking industry.

10 B (small pieces of colored glass were arranged in a pattern around a mold)

11 i Any one point: Quintus would have found the climate of Britain rather inhospitable, compared to both that of his native Italy and that of Alexandria. In the story "tres servi," Unit 2, page 5, the slave Philus complains, "*iterum pluit! semper pluit! nos solem numquam videmus. ego ad Italiam redire volo. ego solem videre volo.*" (lines 3–5). From this it can be inferred that it rains much more in Britain than it does in Italy. Alexandria, like Italy, located on the

Mediterranean Sea, would have had a climate more similar to Italy's—that is, generally sunny and temperate, with a relatively brief rainy season.

ii When the Romans invaded Britain, they found society there in a relatively primitive state of advancement, compared to their own country. The economy was mainly agricultural, and there was little contact with other parts of the world. Salvius' complaints about the Britons particularly reflected these conditions. Alexandria, by contrast, had been dominated by the Greeks for about three hundred years before the arrival of the Romans, so its culture had achieved a level of advancement at least comparable to that of Italy.

12a The founder of Alexandria was Alexander the Great, who was Macedonian and Greek.

12b The Greeks took the credit for the planning and construction of Alexandria (whose architect was, in fact, Greek).

12c Even after the Romans had conquered Alexandria, the Greeks, well established by then, continued to wield considerable power and influence: they took part in administration of the government, theirs was the official language, they commanded a great deal of the city's wealth, and they were, in general, a privileged class. Presumably the native Egyptians resented the co-optation of the city by two non-native groups, and one consequence of this resentment was that uprisings occurred, such as the attack by a group of Egyptians disaffected with both the Greeks and the Romans on the house of the Greek Diogenes, depicted in the story "tumultus," Unit 2, pages 81–83.

13a Any one point:
– appointing client kings like Cogidubnus to influence their own people into remaining submissive.
– sending governors like Agricola to encourage "Romanization"—speaking Latin, Roman style of housing, clothing, etc.
– building roads to let troops move more quickly and suppress revolts.
– the system of forts, etc., in strategic locations where trouble might be brewing.

13b Any three points:
– Roman, not British, gods are named in the dedication.
– "the divine house" is an admission of the Roman-induced belief in the divinity of the Emperor.
– the "safety of the divine house" involves praying for the welfare of a foreign ruler—the Emperor.
– the lettering on the inscription is professional—either a craftsman imported from Italy or one trained to imitate the Roman style—either way admitting the supremacy of anything Roman.

25 points for Part B
Total: 75 points

PART A Understanding the story

Read the following story, and then answer the questions based on it.
Answer all questions on the Answer Sheets provided.

somnium Clēmentis

rēx Cogidubnus, cum Quīntō in aulae hortō ambulāns et dē morte Barbillī dīcēns, fidem iuvenis laudābat:

"mī amīce, tū es vir fidēlissimus. prīmō vītam meam servāvistī. nunc dē morte Barbillī, amīcī patris tuī, et dē itinere tuō ad hanc īnsulam cognōscō. dīc mihi! tūne ad Britanniam vēnistī, quod Rūfum, fīlium Barbillī, invenīre voluistī?"

"Barbillus, priusquam periit, hoc rogāvit," respondit Quīntus.

"sī hoc facere nōn potes," perrēxit rēx, "tū hērēs Barbillī es?"

"ita vērō!"

"rem mīrābilem facis!" Cogidubnus exclāmāvit. "paucī Rōmānī, paucī Britannī, paucī hominēs tam fidēlēs sunt. nōnne dītissimus esse potes, sī hunc Rūfum invenīre nōn potes? tū tamen eum quaerere pērgis!"

"hic Rūfus, sīcut ego, patrem āmīsit," explicāvit Quīntus. "necesse est mihi fīlium quaerere, quod pater meus hoc mē docuit, et quod pater eius hoc mihi crēdidit. nōlī autem attonitus esse! nōn difficile est Rūfum invenīre. Gāius Salvius Līberālis enim, apud quem nunc habitō, multōs mīlitēs Rōmānōs cognōvit. nōnne ille mē adiuvāre potest?

"Quīntus Caecilius Clēmēns quoque, lībertus meus, quī in urbe Alexandrīā manet, ubi ab Aegyptō discēdēbam, mihi spem magnam dedit. nam ā templō Īsidis rediēns, ubi deae precēs dē salūte meā adhibuerat, mihi dē somniō mīrābilī nārrāvit. in hōc somniō, quod dea Īsis ipsa mīserat, Clēmēns rēgem vīdit, quī senex erat. inimīcī, quī rēgī invidēbant, eum necāre temptābant. ego, postquam rēgem adiūvī, praemium magnum accēpī . . . Rūfum invēnī!"

rēx, quī fābulam vix crēdere poterat, paene lacrimābat.

"ego sum senex," inquit, "quem adiuvistī! nunc praemium exspectās, et praemium merēs! deam Īsidem nescio, sed tē bene iam cognōvī. tū Rūfum invenīre potes!"

somnium, somniī, n.	*dream*
fides, fideī, f.	*trustworthiness, honesty*
prīmō	*first*
priusquam	*before*
sī	*if*
pērgō, pērgere, perrēxī	*continue*
hērēs, hērēdis, m.f.	*heir*
dītissimus	*very rich*
explicō, explicāre, explicāvī	*explain*
doceō, docēre, docuī	*teach*
autem	*but, however*
enim	*for*
adiuvō, adiuvāre, adiūvī	*help, assist*
spēs, speī, f.	*hope*
salūs, salūtis, f.	*safety*
adhibeō, adhibēre, adhibuī	*offer*
invideō, invidēre	*envy, be jealous of*
praemium, praemiī, n.	*reward*
mereō, merēre	*deserve*
nescio, nescīre	*not know*

PART A Understanding the story

Answer all questions on the Answer Sheets provided.
Answer in complete English sentences (unless otherwise instructed).

1a Where did the conversation in this story take place?

1b What event was King Cogidubnus talking about at the beginning of the story?

1c What opinion of Quintus did he express?

2 One reason Cogidubnus gave for holding this opinion is found in the sentence: *vītam meam servāvistī.* (line 3)

2a Translate the sentence into English.

2b From your memory of the stories in Stages 13–16, give three details from the event to which Cogidubnus is referring here.

3a Translate Cogidubnus' question in lines 5–6: "*tūne ad Britanniam vēnistī, quod Rūfum, fīlium Barbillī, invenīre voluistī?*"

3b According to Quintus' answer in line 7, why did he take on this task?

3c What did the King realize would happen if Quintus could not complete his task successfully?

3d In his comments beginning with "*rem mīrābilem facis!*" the King explained why he found Quintus' behavior *mīrābilem*. Translate the question: "*nōnne dītissimus esse potes sī hunc Rūfum invenīre nōn potes?*" (lines 11–12)

3e In the sentence beginning "*paucī Rōmānī . . .*" (lines 10–11) Cogidubnus indicates what is *mīrābilem* about Quintus' behavior. What is Cogidubnus' reason for admiring Quintus?

4a Why did Quintus feel a certain sympathy for Rufus?

4b What reason did Quintus add (lines 14–16) to the one he gave earlier (the answer to 3b) for taking on his task?

4c What explanation did Quintus give Cogidubnus to suggest that the task would not be too difficult? (lines 16–19)

5 Quintus finished his explanation by telling Cogidubnus about a dream. (lines 20–26)

5a Who had had the dream?

5b What other information about this man did Quintus remind Cogidubnus of?

5c When had this man told Quintus about this dream? (line 21)

5d Where had this man been just before telling Quintus about this dream?

5e Why had he gone there?

5f Who had sent the dream? (lines 22–24)

5g Whom had the man seen in the dream? (line 24)

5h What important detail was mentioned about the person who was seen in the dream?

5i What was happening to this person?

5j Why was it happening?

5k What role did Quintus play in the dream?

5l What happened to Quintus as a result?

6a What was the King's reaction when he heard the dream? (line 27)

6b What prediction did he make?

6c What reason did he give for making that prediction?

7 From the story, select and write in Latin one example of:

i a noun in the vocative case
ii a present participle
iii a verb in the imperative mood
iv a verb in the pluperfect tense
v a relative pronoun in the accusative case
vi an adjective in the superlative degree

8 Which Latin words in the story provide the roots for the following English words?

i imprecation
ii itinerary
iii paucity
iv volition

50 points for Part A

PART B Understanding the background

Answer all questions on the Answer Sheets provided.
Answer in complete English sentences (unless otherwise instructed).

1 King Cogidubnus, whose conversation with Quintus is recorded in the story, was a "client king" in Britain, under Roman rule.

1a What was one duty Cogidubnus had, as a client king?

1b What was one privilege he was granted, as a client king?

1c Cogidubnus' tribe had once been called the Atrebates. What new name was given to the tribe when its leader, Cogidubnus, became the Romans' client king?

1d Cogidubnus was an historical character. What is one proof we have that Cogidubnus really existed?

2 This picture shows Cogidubnus and Quintus together.

2a Where are Cogidubnus and Quintus in this picture?

2b In what modern British village is that site now located?

2c The plants in the foreground may be roses. What proof have archaeologists found that roses might have been grown on the site?

2d Give two other details of the site that archaeologists have discovered and/or re-created for visitors to see.

3a Which Roman emperor brought Britain into the Roman Empire?

3b What was one possible reason for his doing so?

3c What was one advantage to the Romans of having Britain as part of their empire?

4 Quintus mentioned Clemens and the city of Alexandria in his conversation with Cogidubnus.

4a In what well-known Alexandrian business was Clemens engaged?

4b What was one other commodity which Rome imported in quantity from Egypt?

4c What was one problem the Romans encountered in the city of Alexandria?

4d In running the whole province of Egypt, what were two limitations (inherited from their predecessors) that Romans imposed on Egyptian peasants?

5 Worship of the Egyptian goddess Isis, also mentioned in the conversation, is illustrated in this picture.

5a In the picture, identify the objects being held by the two figures in the right foreground.

5b What are two other features of the worship ceremony for Isis which you could suggest, based on the clues in this picture?

5c What is one of the beliefs about Isis mentioned in either the stories or the cultural material of Unit 2, Stages 17–20?

6 Barbillus, who is discussed in the conversation, received expert medical treatment from Petro, the doctor in Stages 17–20.

6a The following pictures give clues to some of the fairly sophisticated medical techniques practiced in the Greco-Egyptian world of Alexandria. Suggest three such techniques illustrated in these pictures.

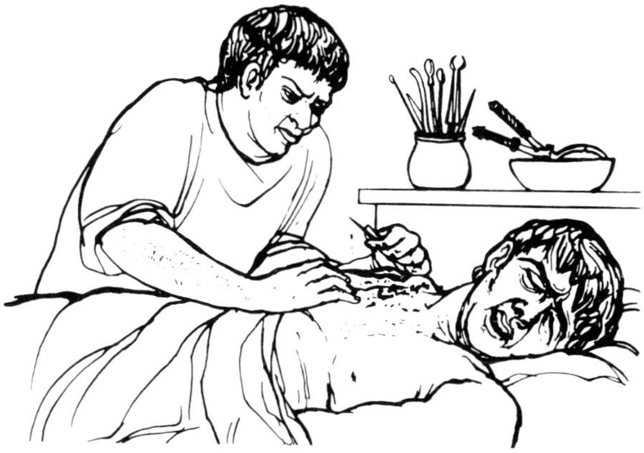

6b Why was Alexandria a better center for the study of anatomy than Greece?

25 points for Part B
Total: 75 points

NOMEN ....

PART A **Understanding the story**

Answer all questions on these sheets.
Answer in complete English sentences (unless otherwise instructed).

1a ____________________ 1

1b ____________________ 1

1c ____________________ 1

2a ____________________ 2

2b ____________________

____

____

____________________ 3

3a ____________________

____

____________________ 5

3b ____________________ 1

3c ____________________ 1

3d ____________________

____________________ 4

3e ____________________ 1

4a ____________________ 1

4b ____________________ 1

4c ____________________

____________________ 2

5a ____________________ 1

NOMEN ....

5b ______________________________ ☐ 1

5c ______________________________ ☐ 1

5d ______________________________ ☐ 1

5e ______________________________ ☐ 1

5f ______________________________ ☐ 1

5g ______________________________ ☐ 1

5h ______________________________ ☐ 1

5i ______________________________ ☐ 1

5j ______________________________ ☐ 1

5k ______________________________ ☐ 1

5l ______________________________ ☐ 1

6a ______________________________

______________________________ ☐ 2

6b ______________________________ ☐ 1

6c ______________________________ ☐ 1

7 i ______________ iv ______________

ii ______________ v ______________

iii ______________ vi ______________ ☐ 6

8 i ______________ iii ______________

ii ______________ iv ______________ ☐ 4

/50 points for Part A

NOMEN ....

PART B **Understanding the background**

Answer all questions on these sheets.
Answer in complete English sentences (unless otherwise instructed).

1a ____

____ ☐ 1

1b ____ ☐ 1

1c ______________________ ☐ 1

1d ____

____ ☐ 1

2a ______________________ ☐ 1

2b ______________________ ☐ 1

2c ____ ☐ 1

2d ____

____

____ ☐ 2

3a ______________________ ☐ 1

3b ____

____ ☐ 1

3c ____

____ ☐ 1

4a ______________________ ☐ 1

4b ______________________ ☐ 1

4c ____ ☐ 1

NOMEN ....

4d ______

______

______ ☐ 2

5a ______ ☐ 1

5b i ______

ii ______ ☐ 2

5c ______

______ ☐ 1

6a i ______

ii ______

iii ______ ☐ 3

6b ______

______ ☐ 1

/25 points for Part B

/50 + /25 = /75 points total

Answer Key

Each question is worth 1 point unless otherwise indicated.

PART A Understanding the story

1a This conversation took place in the garden of the/Cogidubnus' palace.

1b The King was talking about Barbillus' death.

1c The King said Quintus was very loyal, trustworthy, honest, etc.

2a "You saved (1) my life (1)." (2 points total)

2b Any three details: At a banquet (1) Belimicus angrily hit a bear (2) when provoked by Dumnorix (1); the bear went out of control (1) and headed towards the King (1); Dumnorix tried unsuccessfully to stop the bear (1); Quintus hurled a spear (1) and killed the bear (1). (3 points total)

3a "Have you come to Britain (2) because you wanted (1) to find (1) Rufus, the son of Barbillus (1)?" (5 points total)

3b Quintus took on this task because Barbillus asked him to.

3c Quintus would be Barbillus' heir.

3d "Surely (1) you can be very rich (1), [You can be very rich, can't you,] if you cannot find (1) this Rufus (1)?" (4 points total)

3e Few men would have done what Quintus had done.

4a They had both lost their fathers.

4b One detail: Quintus' father had taught him to behave this way. Barbillus trusted him.

4c Any two points: Salvius, at whose house he was staying, knew many soldiers, and could help find Rufus. (2 points)

5a Clemens had had this dream.

5b Clemens was a freedman; he was still in Alexandria.

5c Clemens told this dream as Quintus was leaving Alexandria (for Britain).

5d Clemens had been at the temple of Isis.

5e He had gone there to pray for Quintus' safety.

5f The goddess Isis had sent the dream.

5g Clemens, in his dream, had seen a king.

5h This king was old / an old man.

5i Enemies were trying to kill him.

5j They were jealous of him.

5k Quintus helped the king.

5l As a result (as a reward) Quintus found Rufus.

6a The King could scarcely believe the story and he was almost in tears. (2 points)

6b The King predicted that Quintus would (could) find Rufus.

6c One detail: Quintus deserved to. Cogidubnus knew Quintus well.

7
- i *amice* (line 3)
- ii *ambulans* (line 1), *dicens* (line 2), *rediens* (line 22)
- iii *dic* (line 5), *noli* (*esse*) (line 16)
- iv *adhibuerat* (line 23), *miserat* (line 24)
- v *quem* (line 17)
- vi *fidelissimus* (line 3), *ditissimus* (line 11) (6 points total)

8 i *preces* (line 22)
ii *itinere* (line 4)
iii *pauci* (lines 10 & 11)
iv *voluisti* (line 6) (4 points total)

50 points for Part A

PART B Understanding the background

1a Any one detail: A client king would collect taxes. He would keep peace in his part of Britain.

1b Any one detail: A client king would be given Roman citizenship, could add the emperor's names to his own, have a grand palace.

1c the Regnenses (This must be spelled correctly.)

1d We know Cogidubnus really existed because the "Neptune and Minerva" dedication stone includes (part of) his name. OR Tacitus (or a Roman historian) mentioned his name (in the *Agricola*).

2a Cogidubnus and Quintus are in (the garden of) the palace.

2b Fishbourne

2c The archaeologists have found holes for stakes to hold climber roses.

2d Any two details: The central path was paved with chippings (gravel). There were lawns on either side and paths around the outside of the lawns. There were beds for shrubs and flowers along the edges of the paths. There were trenches for special bedding soil for the flowers and shrubs. There were underground pipes for water to the fountains. There were small marble and bronze statues placed at intervals. (2 points)

3a Claudius

3b He needed a prestigious victory. OR He had new information of British wealth.

3c Any one: From Britain the Romans could have a source of slaves, metals, grain, revenues, hunting dogs, new customers for Roman merchandise, protection of the empire's northwest flank.

4a Clemens was a shopkeeper, selling glass.

4b Any one: Rome imported wheat/papyrus from Egypt.

4c Racial tension / riots / resentment on the part of the local inhabitants was one problem the Romans had in Alexandria.

4d Any two details: Peasants were not allowed to leave their village without permission; they had to plant whatever crop they were told to; they did not receive their share of the harvest until rulers had theirs. (2 points)

5a sistra (sistrums, sacred rattles)

5b Any two points: Worship of Isis involved sacrifice, garlands on altar, pipes for music, choral singing. (2 points)

5c Any one point: She represented hope of life after death (or any of the details of her relation with Osiris/Horus); she controlled the coming of the spring / good sailing weather / flooding of the Nile / crops.

6a Any three points: Medical techniques included the use of drugs to cure disease. Minor surgery was regularly practiced (e.g. tonsils, even cataracts, amputations). There was insistence on sterilization of equipment or washing-up for doctors (cup for boiling water). Doctors had the ability to tie up veins and arteries, sew up wounds. (3 points)

6b Unlike Greeks, Egyptians did not fear or dislike dissection of corpses (since mummification was practiced).

25 points for Part B
Total: 75 points

PART A Understanding the story

Read the following story, and then answer the questions based on it.
Answer all questions on the Answer Sheets provided.

poena astrologi

Quīntus, postquam Barbillus periit, dē poenā idōneā astrologō, Hōropī, cōgitābat. nam in testāmentō, Barbillus Quīntum astrologum pūnīre iusserat. postrēmō Quīntus ad praedium, quod in testāmentō ā Barbillō accēperat, eum mittere cōnstituit. ibi enim Hōrops nōn iam poterat astrologus esse. nam necesse erat eī in fundō per tōtum diem labōrāre.

quondam Phormiō, quī erat lībertus Quīntī et praediō praeerat, Hōropem in fundō labōrantem cōnspexit. Hōrops erat querulus.

"quam fessus sum!" inquit astrologus. "num decōrum est astrologō fossās effodere?"

subitō Phormiō serpentem ingentem Hōropī appropinquantem vīdit.

"nōlī tē movēre!" clāmāvit Phormiō. "manē in illō locō! serpēns magnus est prope pedem tuum."

subitō sē movēns et effugere temptāns titubāvit astrologus. serpēns eum in crūre percussit. deinde Hōrops exanimātus humī prōcubuit.

servī Hōropem ad vīllam portāvērunt et Phormiō eum cūrābat. vīlicus vulnus secuit et multus sanguis effluēbat. tum postquam sanguis diū efflūxit, Phormiō vulnus, in quō arāneās posuerat, dēligāvit. astrologus versūs magnificōs recitāvit, sed frūstrā. vulnus serpentis ingravēscēbat. venēnum per tōtum crūs eius fluēbat.

Phormiō, quod Hōropī artem medicī dēmōnstrāre voluit, Petrōnem, medicum optimum, quī Barbillum sānāre temptāverat, arcessīvit. Petrō, quod astrologus moritūrus erat, crūs statim amputāvit.

per multōs mēnsēs astrologum cūrābat Petrō. dē arte medicīnae inter sē saepe sermōnēs habēbant. quondam, postquam Hōrops convaluit, sēcum cōgitābat et Petrōnī,

"nunc rem intellegō," inquit. "mortem Barbillō intulī. remedium meum erat pessimum, tuum optimum. stultissimus eram."

poena, poenae, f.	*punishment*
idōneus, idōnea, idōneum	*suitable*
testāmentum, testāmentī, n.	*will*
iubeō, iubēre, iussī	*order*
praedium, praediī, n.	*estate*
cōnstituō, cōnstituere, cōnstituī	*decide*
enim	*for*
nōn iam	*no longer*
querulus, querula, querulum	*complaining*
effodiō, effodere	*dig*
titubō, titubāre, titubāvī	*stumble*
in crūre	*on the leg*
percutiō, percutere, percussī	*strike*
humī	*on the ground*
secō, secāre, secui	*cut*
effluō, effluere	*flow out*
arānea, arāneae, f.	*spider's web*
dēligō, dēligāre, dēligāvī	*tie up*
ingravēscō, ingravēscere	*worsen*
venēnum, venēnī, n.	*poison*
crūs, crūris, n.	*leg*
sānō, sānāre	*heal*
moritūrus, moritūra, moritūrum	*going to die*
mēnsis, mēnsis, m.	*month*
convalēscō, convalēscere, convaluī	*recover, recuperate*

PART A Understanding the story

Answer all questions on the Answer Sheets provided.
Answer in complete English sentences (unless otherwise instructed).

1 Why did Quintus punish the astrologer? (lines 2–3)

2 Give two details of that punishment. (lines 3–6)

3 Translate *quam fessus sum!* (line 9)

4 On your Answer Sheet, circle the letter next to the best translation of *num decōrum est astrologō fossās effodere?* (lines 9–10)

A Surely it is not proper for an astrologer to dig ditches?
B Is it proper for an astrologer to dig ditches?
C It is proper, isn't it, for an astrologer to dig ditches?

5 What happened while Horops was complaining? (line 11)

6 What did Phormio shout to the astrologer? (line 12)

7 Why did the snake strike? Give two details. (line 14)

8a Write in **Latin** the sentence that tells you the astrologer's reaction to the snake bite.

8b Translate the sentence into English.

9a What was the first thing anyone did after the accident? (line 16)

9b List three steps that Phormio took to help Horops. (lines 17–18)

9c How did the astrologer try to help his own situation? (line 19)

10 Why did the wound grow worse? (line 20)

11a Whom did Phormio then consult? (lines 21–22)

11b What was his reason for consulting this person?

12 Translate into English the sentence in lines 21–22: *Phormiō, quod Hōropī artem medicī dēmōnstrāre voluit, Petrōnem, medicum optimum, quī Barbillum sānāre temptāverat, arcessīvit.*

13a What medical procedure was next performed? (line 23)

13b On your Answer Sheet, circle the letter of the picture below which shows the kind of medical implements that a *medicus* would have used.

A

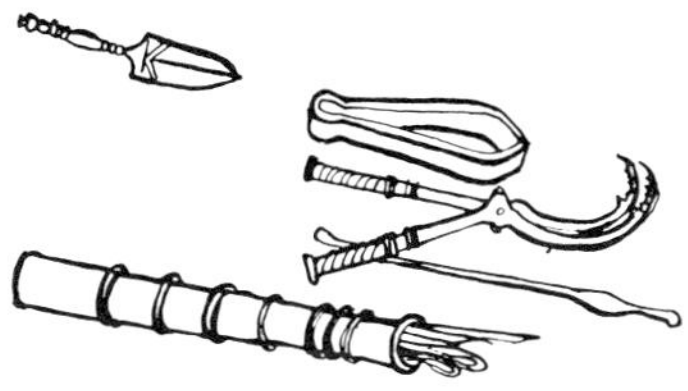

B

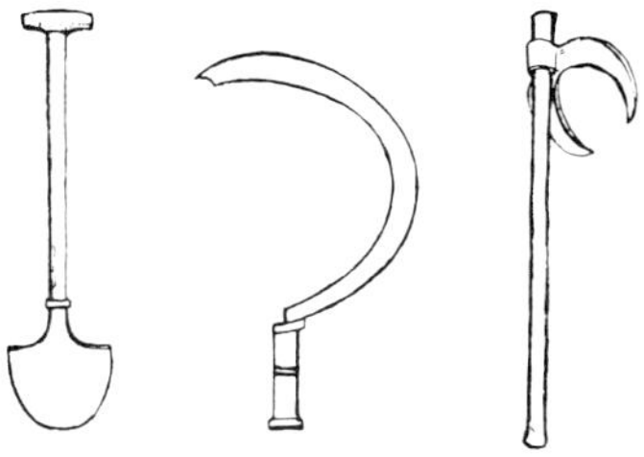

C

14 What did Petro and the astrologer often discuss? (lines 24–25)

15 By the end of the story, how have the astrologer's ideas about medicine changed from when we first met him in Unit 2?

16 Find one example of the pluperfect tense in lines 3–4, and translate it.

17 On your Answer Sheet, circle the correct answer: *labōrāre*, *effodere*, and *esse* are all examples of:

A present participles B infinitives C imperatives

18 Write in **Latin** one command that appears in line 12, and translate it.

19a In lines 12–13, find a noun–adjective pair, write it in **Latin**, and translate it.

19b For the pair you have selected in 19a, give the case, number, and gender.

20 Find an example of a present participle in line 14 and translate it.

21 On your Answer Sheet, circle the correct answer: *serpentis* (line 19) is:

A nominative case B genitive case C dative case

22 What kind of clause is *quī Barbillum sānāre temptāverat*? (line 22)

23 Which word is the subject of *per multōs mēnsēs astrologum cūrābat Petrō*? (line 24)

24 Identify one superlative adjective in line 28, write it in Latin, and translate it.

25 Give the **Latin** words in the story which yield the following derivatives:

i cogitate ii vulnerable iii impunity iv imposition

50 points for Part A

PART B

Understanding the background

Answer all questions on the Answer Sheets provided.
Answer in complete English sentences (unless otherwise instructed).

1 Examine the two pictures on your Answer Sheet.

1a In what country is each of the ceremonies taking place?

1b Tell whom each statue represents.

1c Tell what happens to each of the statues.

1d Explain why each statue is being honored.

2 Here are five commonly noted aspects of Roman religion. Choose the **two** that are illustrated in the pictures for question 1 and, on your Answer Sheet, put the letter (A or B) of the picture beside the aspect it illustrates:

household gods, lares, and penates
Etruscan superstitions, divination
Emperor worship
Romanization of Greek gods
mystery religions, cults

3 For each description below and on your Answer Sheet, put the letter (A or B) of the picture from question 1 that each of these sentences describes:

i *sacerdōtēs statuam deae per viās portant.*
ii *flammae, quae effigiem iam tangēbant, cēram liquēbant.*
iii *subitō aquila ex effigiē ēvolāvit.*

4 Examine the pictures on your Answer Sheet. For each of the pictures:

a identify the building;
b state in what province it was built;
c indicate one similarity to Caecilius' house in Pompeii;
d indicate one difference from Caecilius' house.

5a Name the Roman general who first explored Britain.

5b Give one reason he had for doing so.

5c Name the Macedonian general who selected the site in Egypt upon which Alexandria was to be built.

5d Give one reason he had for doing so.

25 points for Part B
Total: 75 points

NOMEN ....

PART A Understanding the story

Answer all questions on these sheets.
Answer in complete English sentences (unless otherwise instructed).

1 ______________________________ ☐ 1

2 i ______________________________
ii ______________________________ ☐ 2

3 ______________ ☐ 1

4 A B C ☐ 1

5 ______________________________ ☐ 1

6 ______________________________ ☐ 1

7 i ______________________________
ii ______________________________ ☐ 2

8a Latin: ______________________________ ☐ 1

8b English: ______________________________ ☐ 1

9a ______________________________ ☐ 1

9b i ______________________________
ii ______________________________
iii ______________________________ ☐ 3

9c ______________________________ ☐ 1

10 ______________________________ ☐ 1

11a ______________________________ ☐ 1

11b ______________________________ ☐ 1

NOMEN ....

12 ______________________________

____

____

____

______________________________ ☐ 6

13a ______________________________ ☐ 1

13b A B C ☐ 1

14 ______________________________ ☐ 1

15 ______________________________

______________________________ ☐ 1

16 Latin: ______________________

English: ______________________ ☐ 2

17 A B C ☐ 1

18 Latin: ______________________

English: ______________________ ☐ 2

19a Latin: ______________________

English: ______________________ ☐ 2

19b Case: ______________________

Number: ______________________

Gender: ______________________ ☐ 3

20 Latin: ______________________

English: ______________________ ☐ 2

21 A B C ☐ 1

22 ______________________ ☐ 1

23 ______________________ ☐ 1

NOMEN ....

24 Latin: ____________________

English: ____________________ ☐ 2

25 i ____________________ iii ____________________

ii ____________________ iv ____________________ ☐ 4

/50 points for Part A

Answer Key

Each question is worth 1 point unless otherwise indicated.

PART A Understanding the story

1 Quintus punished the astrologer because Barbillus had ordered him to (in his will).

2 The punishment was that he had to work on the farm and could no longer be an astrologer. (2 points)

3 How tired I am!

4 A (Surely it is not proper for an astrologer to dig ditches?)

5 A huge snake approached Horops. / Phormio saw a huge snake approaching Horops.

6 Phormio shouted, "Don't move!" and/or "Stay in that place!"

7 The snake struck because Horops moved suddenly while trying to flee (1), and then tripped (1). (2 points total)

8a *deinde Hōrops exanimātus humī prōcubuit.*

8b Then he fell unconscious on the ground.

9a The slaves carried Horops to the house.

9b Phormio cut the wound (1), placed spiders' webs on it (1), and bound it up (1). (3 points total)

9c The astrologer recited magic verses.

10 The poison flowed through the astrologer's leg.

11a Phormio consulted Petro.

11b Petro was an excellent doctor and/or had tried to heal Barbillus and/or Phormio wanted to show Horops the art of medicine / skill of a doctor.

12 Because Phormio wanted (1) to point out to Horops (1) the art/skill of a doctor (1), he summoned Petro (1), an excellent doctor (1), who had tried to heal Barbillus (1). (6 points total)

13a Petro amputated the astrologer's leg.

13b A

14 They often discussed the art of medicine.

15 The astrologer now knew his methods were wrong and Petro's were correct.

16 *iusserat*: he had ordered; *acceperat*: he had received (2 points)

17 B (infinitives)

18 *noli te movere!*: don't move!; *mane!*: stay! / remain! (2 points)

19a *serpens magnus*: big snake (2 points)

19b nominative (1) singular (1) masculine (1) (3 points total)

20 *movens*: moving; *temptans*: trying (2 points)

21 B (genitive case)

22 a relative clause

23 *Petro*

24 *pessimum*: very bad; *optimum*: very good; *stultissimus*: very stupid (2 points)

25 i *cogitabat* (line 2) ii *vulnus* (line 17) iii *punire* (*poena*) (line 3) iv *posuerat* (line 18)

50 points for Part A

PART B Understanding the background

1a A Egypt
B Britain (2 points)

1b A Isis
B (Emperor) Claudius (2 points)

1c A paraded through streets to harbor / returned to the temple of Isis
B burned on a pyre (2 points)

1d A a festival of Isis in the spring / to open the sailing season
B Claudius made Cogidubnus king (2 points)

2 Emperor worship B
mystery religions, cults A (2 points)

3 i A
ii B
iii B (3 points)

4a A Fishbourne Palace / Cogidubnus' palace
B Barbillus' house (in Alexandria) (2 points)

4b A Britain
B Egypt (2 points)

4c A garden area / slaves' quarters / indoor plumbing / etc.
B impluvium / tablinum / columns in atrium / etc. (2 points)

4d A larger / has its own set of baths
B more lavish / expensive decorations (2 points)

5a Julius Caesar

5b curiosity / desire for fame / to stop British support of the Gauls / he had been told there were metals and other resources worth obtaining there / etc.

5c Alexander (the Great)

5d strategic location on trade routes / good harbor / good supply of building materials / etc.

25 points for Part B
Total: 75 points

PART A Understanding the story

**Read the following story, and then answer the questions based on it.
Answer all questions on the Answer Sheets provided.**

dē tempestāte

Quīntus et Barbillus saepe domum Aristōnis vīsitāre solēbant. Barbillus quondam fābulam mīrābilem nārrāre coepit:

"hic diēs," inquit Barbillus, "dulcior est mihi quam vīta mea quod hodiē ad urbem Alexandrīam revēnit Catullus, amīcus meus, quī est mercātor.

"Catullus, ā Graeciā nāvigāns, Alexandrīae appropinquābat, ubi nūbēs dēnsissima apparuit. deinde undae altissimae per mare tōtum surgēbant, nāvem superantēs. omnēs sollicitī, quī in magnīs undīs perīre nōlēbant, clāmōrem magnum tollēbant. subitō gubernātor cōnsilium cēpit.

" 'mercem tōtam,' inquit, 'in mare iactāre dēbēmus.'

"plūrimī, postquam hoc audīvērunt, cōnsilium laudābant. Catullus tamen, rem graviter ferēns, cōnsiliō resistēbat quod mercem āmittere nōlēbat. paulisper cōgitāns,

" 'difficile est mihi,' inquit, 'mercem tōtam āmittere. prīmō nautae mercem gravissimam in mare iactāre dēbent. gemmās, quae parvae et pretiōsae sunt, servāre valdē cupiō.'

"gubernātor cōnsentiēns nautās iussit amphorās vīnī tollere et in mare iactāre. omnēs amphorās quās invenīre poterant nautae in aquam quam celerrimē iactāvērunt, sed undae ingentēs in nāvem fluēbant. deinde aliās rēs in undās iactāvērunt, sed frūstrā labōrāvērunt. tandem nautae miserī nāvem ipsam frangere coepērunt et partēs nāvis in mare iactāvērunt. Catullus, mortem timēns, gemmās in mare iactāvit et auxilium deōrum petīvit.

"dēnique pharum in portū cōnspexērunt. ad urbem Alexandrīam pervēnerant! fortūnam crūdēlem effūgerant!"

Barbillus, postquam hanc fābulam mīrābilem nārrāvit, amīcīs nūntiāvit,

"nunc necesse est mihi maximās grātiās deīs agere quod amīcum meum servāvērunt. duōs agnōs niveōs ēlēgī et ad templum dūxī ubi sacerdōtēs eōs in ārā sacrificāvērunt."

Galatēa, uxor Aristōnis, quae fābulam audīverat, rogāvit,

"cūr hoc fēcistī? hērēs Catullī nōn es! Catullus trēs fīliōs parvōs habet. quid cupīvistī?"

Barbillus rīdēns Galatēae respondit,

"nihil cupiō. sed, quod amīcus cārissimus vīvit, gaudeō."

tempestās, tempestātis, f.	*storm*
appāreo, appārēre, appāruī	*appear*
altus, alta, altum	*high*
gubernātor, gubernātōris, m.	*helmsman*
merx, mercis, f.	*goods, merchandise*
iactō, iactāre	*throw, toss*
graviter ferō, graviter ferre	*take badly*
prīmō	*first*
gravis	*heavy*
iubeō, iubēre, iussī	*order*
amphora, amphorae, f.	*jar*
quam celerrimē	*as quickly as possible*
pharus, pharī, m.	*lighthouse*
agnus, agnī, m.	*lamb*
niveus, nivea, niveum	*snow-white*
ēligō, ēligere, ēlēgī	*choose*
sacrificō, sacrificāre, sacrificāvī	*sacrifice*
hērēs, hērēdis, m.	*heir*
gaudeō, gaudēre	*rejoice*

PART A Understanding the story

Answer all questions on the Answer Sheets provided.
Answer in complete English sentences (unless otherwise instructed).

1a Whose house was Barbillus visiting when he told this story? (line 1)

1b In line 2 find a noun–adjective pair, write it in **Latin**, and translate it into English.

2a Why did that particular day mean so much to Barbillus? (line 4)

2b Who was the merchant? (lines 4–5)

3 What case is *Alexandrīae*? (line 6)

4a What effect were the waves having in lines 7–8?

4b On your Answer Sheet circle the letter of the correct description of *superantēs*, in line 8:

A infinitive B noun C present participle

5 In lines 8–9 find a relative clause, write it in **Latin**, and translate it into English.

6 What was the helmsman's plan? (line 11)

7a Who praised the helmsman's plan? (line 12)

7b How did Catullus react to the plan? (lines 12–13)

7c Why did Catullus react this way? (lines 13–14)

8a What did Catullus think the sailors should do first? (lines 15–16)

8b What did he want to keep? (lines 16–17)

8c Why did he think that this would not endanger the ship? (line 16)

8d Examine the following sentence: *gemmās, quae parvae et pretiōsae sunt, servāre valdē cupiō*. On your Answer Sheet **underline** the relative clause, **circle** the relative pronoun and **draw a box** around the noun to which it refers.

9 On your Answer Sheet circle the letter that describes all of the following: *servāre*, *āmittere*, *iactāre*, and *perīre*:

A present participles B infinitives C imperatives

10a What did the helmsman order first? (lines 18–19)

10b To indicate whether his order was carried out, translate the following (from lines 19–20) into English:

omnēs amphorās quās invenīre poterant nautae in aquam quam celerrimē iactāvērunt.

10c What adjective describes *undae*? (line 20)

10d What case is *undae*? (line 20)

11a What did the sailors try next? (line 21)

11b Which **Latin** word in line 21 tells you how successful their efforts were?

12a Which **Latin** word in line 22 describes how the sailors felt at this point?

12b What did the sailors try in desperation? (lines 22–23)

13a Find a two-word phrase in line 23 that describes how Catullus felt. Write it in Latin, and then translate it into English.

13b What two things did Catullus do next? (lines 23–24)

13c What case is *deōrum*? (line 24)

14 How did the people on the ship know that they had reached Alexandria? (line 25)

15 What tense is *pervēnerant*? (line 26)

16a Translate into English: *nunc necesse est mihi maximās grātiās deīs agere.* (line 29)

16b Why did Barbillus think he should take the action described in the sentence you translated in question 16a, above? (lines 29–30)

16c How did he go about doing it? (lines 30–31)

17a Translate into English: *cūr hoc fēcistī?* (line 33)

17b Based on the rest of her comments, what reason did Galatea have for saying this? (lines 33–34)

17c What did Barbillus reply? (line 36)

18 Which **Latin** words in the story yield the following derivatives?

- i cogitate
- ii frangible
- iii propinquity
- iv undulate

50 points for Part A

PART B Understanding the background

Answer all questions on the Answer Sheets provided.
Answer in complete English sentences (unless otherwise instructed).

1 On your Answer Sheet, circle the letter that names the people who, on the death of Alexander the Great, ruled Alexandria:

A Egyptians B Romans
C Greeks D Jews

2 Which of the following items would **not** have been included as a possible cargo on the ship from Athens to Alexandria?

A grain B timber
C marble D copper

3 The lighthouse mentioned in the story was famous

A as a monument to Isis
B as one of the Seven Wonders of the Ancient World
C as a symbol of Roman authority
D as a burial tomb for the Pharaohs

4 The Caesareum where Barbillus made his offering was begun by

A Alexander the Great B Cleopatra
C Marcus Antonius D the Emperor Augustus

5 Which one of the following men did **not** study at Alexandria?

A Hippocrates B Herophilus
C Euclid D Eratosthenes

6 Egypt was the center of worship for the goddess Isis and her son, whose name was

A Serapis B Horus
C Mithras D Osiris

7 A temple of Isis has also been discovered in Britain at

A Aquae Sulis B Fishbourne
C London D Chichester

8 Cogidubnus, the British king, is mentioned on a temple inscription in Britain. The temple where his name appeared was dedicated to Minerva and

A Sulis B Juno
C Jupiter D Neptune

9 Cogidubnus was made king by the Emperor

A Augustus B Claudius
C Vespasian D Domitian

10 The tribe which Cogidubnus headed was called the

A Regnenses B Durotriges
C Cantiaci D Iceni

11 Name **two** products which the Romans imported from Egypt.

12 Name **two** products which the Romans imported from Britain.

13 Give one significant piece of information about any **three** of the following places in Alexandria:

A Cleopatra's Needles B the Museum
C the Royal Quarter D Canopus Street

14 Give one significant piece of information about any **two** of the following persons, connected with Roman Britain:

A Gnaeus Iulius Agricola B Boudica C Aulus Plautius

15 Ctesibius, Hero, and Eratosthenes were responsible for the technological achievements pictured below. **First,** write the name of the man responsible (short answer). **Then,** explain in a sentence or two what each figure represents. In other words, what exactly was the scientific achievement that each diagram shows?

A

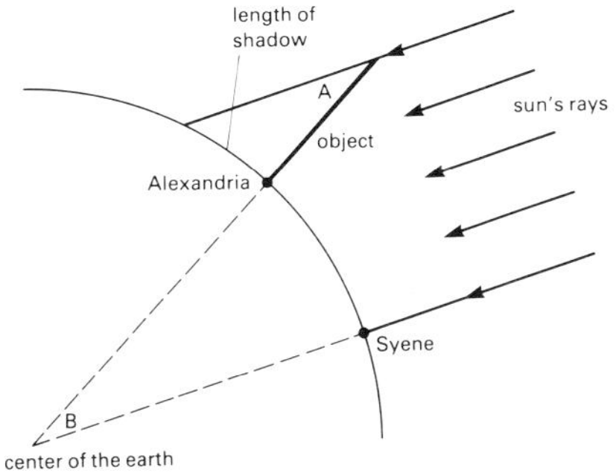

B

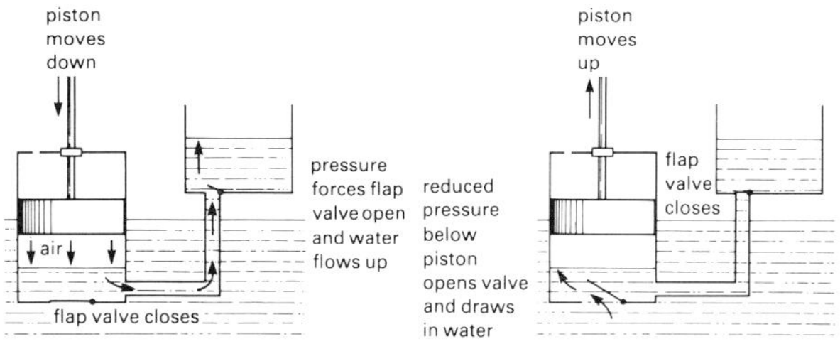

C

25 points for Part B
Total: 75 points

NOMEN ....

PART A **Understanding the story**

Answer all questions on these sheets.
Answer in complete English sentences (unless otherwise instructed).

1a ______________________________ ☐ 1

1b Latin: ______________________

English: ______________________ ☐ 2

2a ______________________________ ☐ 1

2b ______________________ ☐ 1

3 ______________________ ☐ 1

4a ______________________________

______________________________ ☐ 1

4b A B C ☐ 1

5 Latin: ______________________________

____

English: ______________________________

______________________________ ☐ 3

6 ______________________________

______________________________ ☐ 1

7a ______________________________ ☐ 1

7b ______________________________ ☐ 1

7c ______________________________ ☐ 1

8a ______________________________

______________________________ ☐ 1

8b ______________________ ☐ 1

NOMEN ....

8c ______________________ 1

8d *gemmas, quae parvae et pretiosae sunt, servare valde cupio.* 3

9 A B C 1

10a ______________________

______________________ 1

10b ______________________

____

______________________ 3

10c ______________ 1

10d ______________ 1

11a ______________________ 1

11b Latin: ______________ 1

12a Latin: ______________ 1

12b ______________________ 1

13a Latin: ______________

English: ______________ 2

13b i ______________________

ii ______________________ 2

13c ______________ 1

14 ______________________ 1

15 ______________ 1

NOMEN ....

16a ______________________________

____

______________________________ ☐ 2

16b ______________________________ ☐ 1

16c ______________________________ ☐ 1

17a ______________________________ ☐ 1

17b ______________________________

____

______________________________ ☐ 1

17c ______________________________

____

______________________________ ☐ 1

18 i ______________ iii ______________

ii ______________ iv ______________ ☐ 4

/50 points for Part A

NOMEN ....

PART B

Understanding the background

Answer all questions on these sheets.
Answer in complete English sentences (unless otherwise instructed).

1 A B C D ☐ 1

2 A B C D ☐ 1

3 A B C D ☐ 1

4 A B C D ☐ 1

5 A B C D ☐ 1

6 A B C D ☐ 1

7 A B C D ☐ 1

8 A B C D ☐ 1

9 A B C D ☐ 1

10 A B C D ☐ 1

11 i ______________________________

ii ______________________________ ☐ 2

12 i ______________________________

ii ______________________________ ☐ 2

13 i ____

____

ii ____

____

iii ____

____ ☐ 3

NOMEN ....

14 i ______________________________

ii ______________________________

______________________________ ☐ 2

15a i ______________________________

ii ______________________________

____

______________________________ ☐ 2

15b i ______________________________

ii ______________________________

____

______________________________ ☐ 2

15c i ______________________________

ii ______________________________

____

______________________________ ☐ 2

/25 points for Part B

/50 + /25 = /75 points total

Answer Key

Each question is worth 1 point unless otherwise indicated.

PART A Understanding the story

1a Barbillus was visiting Aristo's house.

1b *fabulam mirabilem*: a marvelous/wonderful/strange story (2 points)

2a That day Barbillus' friend (Catullus) returned to Alexandria.

2b Catullus was the merchant.

3 dative

4a The waves were (swelling all through the sea and) overpowering the ship.

4b C (present participle)

5 *qui in magnis undis perire nolebant* (1): who did not wish to die (1) in the great waves (1) (3 points total)

6 The helmsman thought that they (the sailors) should toss all of the goods into the sea.

7a Very many (people) praised the helmsman's plan.

7b Catullus took it very badly AND/OR he was resisting the plan.

7c He did not want to lose his merchandise.

8a He thought they should first throw the heaviest merchandise into the sea.

8b Catullus wanted to keep the jewels.

8c The jewels were small.

8d *gemmas*, *quae parvae et pretiosae sunt, servare valde cupio.* (3 points total)

9 B (infinitives)

10a The helmsman ordered the sailors to lift up the wine-jars and toss them into the sea.

10b The sailors threw all the wine-jars they could (were able to) find into the water as quickly as possible. [*omnes amphoras . . . in aquam* (1 point) *quas invenire poterant* (1) *nautae . . . quam celerrime iactaverunt* (1)] (3 points total)

10c *ingentes*

10d nominative

11a They threw other things into the sea.

11b *frustra*

12a *miseri*

12b They began to break up the ship and throw parts of it into the sea.

13a *mortem timens*: fearing death (2 points)

13b i He threw his jewels into the sea.

ii He sought (begged for) the help of the gods. (2 points total)

13c genitive

14 They saw the lighthouse.

15 pluperfect

16a "Now it is necessary for me (1) to give the greatest (very great) thanks to the gods (1)." (2 points total)

16b The gods had saved Barbillus' friend.

16c Any one detail: He took two white lambs to the temple to be sacrificed. (Students need not mention the priests.)

17a "Why did you do this?"

17b Galatea felt that Barbillus had nothing to gain from sacrificing to the gods for Catullus' safety, because he did not stand to inherit anything from Catullus' will.

17c Barbillus replied that he wanted nothing, and that he rejoiced because his very dear friend was alive. (A direct translation is also acceptable as a response to this question.)

18
- i *cogitans* (line 14)
- ii *frangere* (line 22)
- iii *appropinquabat* (line 6)
- iv *undae* (lines 7 & 20); *undis* (line 8); *undas* (line 21)

50 points for Part A

PART B Understanding the background

1 C (Greeks)

2 A (grain)

3 B (as one of the Seven Wonders of the Ancient World)

4 B (Cleopatra)

5 A (Hippocrates)

6 B (Horus)

7 C (London)

8 D (Neptune)

9 B (Claudius)

10 A (Regnenses)

11 Any two of the following: glass, wheat, papyrus, clothing, perfumes, spices. (2 points)

12 Any two of the following: grain, hunting dogs, iron, gold, tin, lead. (2 points)

13–14 The following are some possible responses to the various parts of the next two questions, but there may of course be other answers that teachers will find acceptable.

13 Any one detail about each of the three places chosen: *Cleopatra's Needles*: Two granite obelisks were brought to Alexandria from an ancient Egyptian temple at Heliopolis. They were placed in front of the Caesareum by a Roman engineer (in 13 B.C.). One of the obelisks is now in London (on the bank of the river Thames), and the other is in (Central Park) New York City.
The Museum was actually a university, which housed the largest library in the ancient world. This was a center of scholarly research where many scholars were employed in a wide range of subjects from mathematics to literature. (Students might mention specific achievements made at the Museum, such as the advances in medicine by Herophilus, etc.)
The Royal Quarter of Alexandria was (more than one square mile (260 hectares)) located by the Great Harbor on the northeast side of the city. It contained palaces, temples, gardens, and government offices. The Caesareum was located just to the west of the Royal Quarter.
Canopus Street, the main street of Alexandria, ran on the east–west axis. It was more than 100 feet (30 meters) wide (i.e. wider than any street in Rome and four times the size of any street in Pompeii). It had houses several stories high, and some public buildings made of marble.
(3 points total)

14 Any one detail about each of the two persons chosen: *Gnaeus Iulius Agricola*, a Roman military man, was governor of Britain from A.D. 78 to 84. He led a number of important military campaigns, and eventually subjugated the Scots. He was noted for being a governor who tried to promote peace and instill in his conquered people an appreciation for the benefits of Roman civilization, e.g. by promoting public building projects and educating the British nobility (in particular, instructing them in the Latin language).
Boudica was a British queen (of the Iceni) in the eastern part of Britain, who bitterly resisted the Roman occupation of her country. She led a fierce revolt in A.D. 61 that constituted a serious

setback for the Romans, but was ultimately crushed. Queen Boudica's rebellion was precipitated by Roman legionaries' rape of her daughters and flogging of Boudica herself after her husband's death. Boudica killed herself by poison, following the defeat of her army, rather than submit to enslavement and further humiliation by the Romans.
Aulus Plautius was commander (under the Emperor Claudius) of the first Roman invasion of Britain. He was the first Roman governor of Britain. (2 points total)

15a i Eratosthenes
ii By applying certain mathematical (geometric) principles, Eratosthenes was able to calculate the earth's circumference (at 24,662 miles, close to the actual figure of 24,857 miles). [See also page 157 of Unit 2.] (2 points total)

15b i Ctesibius
ii This figure represents the flap valve and force pump invented by Ctesibius, which was used in the construction of the first musical organ (*hydraulis*, or water-flute). [Students with a good memory for mechanical detail may include the description of how this device worked, found on page 158 of Unit 2.] (2 points total)

15c i Hero
ii Hero invented the first steam turbine. It was originally a toy, consisting of a hollow ball mounted on two brackets on the lid of a container of boiling water. This device was constructed in such a way that the force of the steam caused the ball to spin around. [Again, students may provide more or less technical descriptions, depending on their aptitude for and interest in science and mechanics. See pages 156–57 of Unit 2.] (2 points total)

25 points for Part B
Total: 75 points

PART A Understanding the story

Read the following story, and then answer the questions based on it. Answer all questions on the Answer Sheets provided.

in viīs Alexandrīae

Phormiō quondam Quīntum ad partem urbis prope templum Serāpidis dūxit. Quīntō omnēs tabernās dēmōnstrāre volēbat. haec pars urbis erat valdē turbulenta et perīculōsa, quod ibi habitābant paucī Graecī. multī tabernāriī gemmās pretiōsās, sērica, vitrea, statuās argenteās cibumque vendēbant. postquam ad hanc partem advēnērunt, difficile erat Quīntō ambulāre per viās quod multī Alexandrīnī eī obstābant. suum comitem vix audīre poterat.

subitō senex Quīntum trūsit. Quīntus et Phormiō erant attonitī.

"cūr illud fēcistī?" rogāvit senem Phormiō.

"ecce!" inquit senex.

magna amphora dē fenestrā dēciderat et in terrā iacēbat ubi steterat Quīntus. tum Quīntus et Phormiō rem intellēxērunt.

"quam benignus es!" Quīntus senī dīxit et eī grātiās ēgit.

"bonam fortūnam habeō," Quīntus sibi dīxit.

per viam ambulantēs, Plancum appropinquantem vīdērunt.

"ēheu!" inquit Quīntus. "cum Plancō dīcere nōlō. necesse est nōbīs quam celerrimē hanc tabernam intrāre."

Phormiō libenter cōnsēnsit; itaque duo comitēs ad tabernam sē vertērunt. Quīntus tamen tabernārium, quī ē suā tabernā discēdēbat, nōn vīdit. Quīntus et tabernārius ad terram prōcubuērunt. Quīntus anxius erat, quod hic tabernārius, quī saeviēbat, ingēns erat vehementerque clāmābat. tabernārius tamen, ubi Phormiōnem cōnspexit, subitō rīsit.

"mī amīce," inquit, "tē agnōscō. dominus tuus est dīvitissimus. gemma, quam in tabernā meā heri ēmit, pretiōsa erat. num comes tuus mē trūdere in animō habēbat? venīte in tabernam meam!"

quamquam tabernārius eōs in tabernam suam invītāverat, Quīntus et Phormiō eī nōn crēdēbant. prōcessērunt igitur per viās. quod fessī erant, ad aliam tabernam īre et vīnum bibere cōnstituērunt. in hāc tabernā habitābat fēlēs pulchra quae omnēs dēlectābat. tabernam intrāns, Quīntus forte caudam huius fēlis calcāvit. fēlēs ululāvit et pedem Quīntī ferōciter rāsit. multus sanguis fluēbat. Quīntus miser clāmāvit,

"auxilium mihi date!"

caupō servum vocāvit et sollicitus dīxit,

"medicus sōlus hoc vulnus cūrāre potest. festīnā! arcesse medicum!"

mox medicus, quī prope tabernam habitābat, advēnit. ille pedem lāvit medicāmentumque ad vulnus applicāvit; dēnique pedem fasciā dēligāvit.

"Quīnte," inquit Phormiō, "tū es valdē fortūnātus! amphora tē nōn vulnerāvit. tabernārius īrātus tē nōn pulsāvit. fēlēs tē graviter nōn rāsit. nōnne dea Īsis tē servāvit?"

Quīntus respondit: "minimē! ego fortūnātus sum quod senex amphoram cōnspexit, quod dominus tuus gemmam ēmit, et quod medicus prope tabernam habitābat."

sērica	*silken goods*
vitrea	*glassware*
comes, comitis, m.	*companion*
trūdō, trūdere, trūsī	*push, shove*
fenestra, fenestrae, f.	*window*
quam celerrimē	*as quickly as possible*
dīves (*gen.* dīvitis)	*rich*
in animō habeō, habēre	*intend, have in mind*
cōnstituō, cōnstituere	*decide*
fēlēs, fēlis, f.	*cat*
cauda, caudae, f.	*tail*
huius (*genitive case of* hic)	
calcō, calcāre, calcāvī	*step on*
ululō, ululāre, ululāvī	*howl*
rādō, rādere, rāsī	*scratch*
caupō, caupōnis, m.	*innkeeper*
medicāmentum, medicāmentī, n.	*medicine*
applicō, applicāre, applicāvī	*apply*
fasciā dēligō, dēligāre, dēligāvī	*tie with a bandage*

PART A Understanding the story

Answer all questions on the Answer Sheets provided.
Answer in complete English sentences (unless otherwise instructed).

1a Where did Phormio take Quintus? (lines 1–2)

1b Why did he do this?

2 From the information given in lines 2–5 tell two things which describe this part of the city.

3 Name one thing besides silk and glass which could be bought there.

4 Explain why Quintus and Phormio were *attonitī*. (line 8)

5 What did the old man **do** to deserve Quintus' thanks? (lines 11–12)

6 What did Quintus say to the old man after the incident described in line 11? Write the Latin sentence and then translate it into English.

7 Why did Quintus suggest they go into a shop? (lines 15–17)

8 Why do you think Quintus and the shopkeeper fell? (lines 19–20)

9 Translate into English the sentence in lines 20–22: *Quīntus anxius erat, quod hic tabernārius, quī saeviēbat, ingēns erat vehementerque clāmābat.*

10a What did the shopkeeper **do** when he caught sight of Phormio? (lines 22–23)

10b Why did he do this?

11 What did the shopkeeper say about Barbillus? (lines 24–25)

12 Why did Quintus and Phormio not accept the shopkeeper's invitation? (lines 27–28)

13 *in hāc tabernā habitābat fēlēs pulchra quae omnēs dēlectābat.* (lines 29–30) "In this shop lived a beautiful cat . . ." Complete the English translation for this Latin sentence.

14 Explain why *multus sanguis fluēbat.* (line 32)

15 Who went to get the doctor?

16 Why do you think that not all Alexandrians at this time would have agreed with the *caupo*'s statement in line 36: *medicus sōlus hoc vulnus cūrāre potest*?

17 What did the doctor do besides applying medicine and bandaging the wound? (lines 37–39)

18 According to Phormio, in what three ways did Isis protect Quintus? (lines 40–42)

19 How did Quintus explain his good fortune in each situation?

20 On your Answer Sheet circle the letter of the adjective which best describes Quintus throughout this story:

A *parātus* B *invītus* C *neglegēns* D *mendāx*

21 *volēbat* (line 2) means "he wanted." On your Answer Sheet, circle the letter of the word below which means "he wants:"

A *vult* B *voluerat* C *voluit*

22 In lines 2–5 find a noun–adjective pair. Write it in Latin and give its case.

23 In line 1 find an example of the genitive case. Write it in Latin.

24 Translate the following words from lines 6–7: *difficile erat Quīntō ambulāre per viās quod multī Alexandrīnī eī obstābant.*

25 On your Answer Sheet circle the letter that names the tense of *dēciderat* (line 11):

A present B imperfect C perfect D pluperfect

26 Translate *ambulantēs* in line 15, and then give its nominative singular form in Latin.

27 What Latin words in lines 17–19 yield the following English derivatives?

celerity consensus subversion

28 Find the imperative verb in line 26. Write it in Latin and tell whether it is singular or plural.

29 Find the relative pronoun in line 25. Write it in Latin and then give its case.

30 Circle the letter of the best translation of *num comes tuus mē trūdere in animō habēbat?* (lines 25–26):

A Did your companion intend to push me?
B Your companion didn't intend to push me, did he?
C Surely your companion intended to push me?

31a Translate the word *īre* in line 29.

31b Circle the correct grammatical term for this form:

A vocative B infinitive C imperative

50 points for Part A

PART B Understanding the background

Answer all questions on the Answer Sheets provided.
Answer in complete English sentences (unless otherwise instructed).

1 On your Answer Sheet put the letter of the description which matches each person from the history of Roman Britain:

Claudius	A	He led the 2nd Legion against the Durotriges during the Roman invasion of Britain.
Julius Caesar	B	He was the first Roman general to lead troops into Britain (in 55 B.C.).
Agricola	C	He was the most famous governor of Britain and stayed there seven years.
Vespasian	D	He made the decision that the Roman army, under the command of Aulus Plautius, should invade Britain in A.D. 43.

2 The inscription right is from a temple built at the request of King Cogidubnus. According to the inscription, in whose honor was this temple built? (Give two names.)

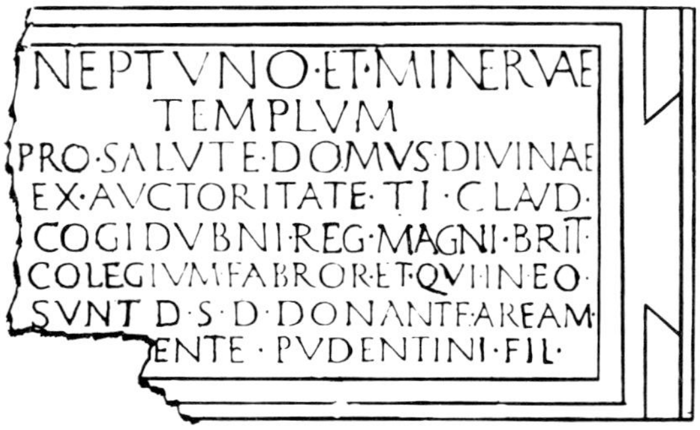

3 Cogidubnus was a "client king." Explain the term "client king."

4 Describe **two** ways in which the palace which has been excavated at Fishbourne was Roman in style.

5 From the point of view of a Briton, indicate one positive aspect of Roman rule.

6 On the map printed on the Answer Sheet, find the place where each of the following events occurred. Place the letter for each statement in the box leading to its correct location.

A *Quīntus et Clēmēns multōs philosophōs audīvit.*
B *Quīntus Clēmentī tabernam ēmit.*
C *mōns Vesuvius Pompēiōs dēlēvit.*
D *Salvius dōnum rēgī Cogidubnō tulit.*

7 What "Wonder of the Ancient World" was located at Alexandria?

8 Why were the Greeks considered the most powerful and influential group in Alexandria?

9 What invention late in the first century B.C. changed the glassmaking industry?

10 The Museum at Alexandria attracted professional scholars doing research in a wide variety of subjects. Beside the name of each scholar, write the letter of his discovery or area of research:

Euclid	A	astronomy
Eratosthenes	B	geometry
Hero	C	anatomy
	D	steam turbine

11 The Alexandrians did not take advantage of their scientific discoveries to build complicated and powerful machines for use in industry. Suggest a reason for this.

12 How did the Egyptian attitude toward the human body make Alexandria a good place to study anatomy?

13 What did the Egyptians believe the goddess Isis could do for them?

14 The object pictured below was associated with the worship of the goddess Isis. Give its Latin name and its use.

25 points for Part B
Total: 75 points

NOMEN ....

PART A

Understanding the story

Answer all questions on these sheets.
Answer in complete English sentences (unless otherwise instructed).

1a ______________________________ 1

1b ______________________________ 1

2 ______________________________

____

______________________________ 2

3 ______________ 1

4 ______________________________ 1

5 ______________________________

______________________________ 1

6 Latin: ______________

English: ______________ 2

7 ______________________________ 1

8 ______________________________

______________________________ 1

9 ______________________________

____

______________________________ 3

10a ______________________________ 1

10b ______________________________ 1

11 ______________________________

______________________________ 1

NOMEN ....

12 ____

____ ☐ 1

13 "In this shop lived a beautiful cat ____________________

____

____ ☐ 1

14 ____ ☐ 1

15 ______________________ ☐ 1

16 ____

____ ☐ 1

17 ____ ☐ 1

18 ____

____

____ ☐ 3

19 ____

____

____

____ ☐ 3

20 A B C D ☐ 1

21 A B C ☐ 1

22 Noun–adjective pair in Latin: ____________________

Case: ______________________ ☐ 2

23 Genitive case: ______________________ ☐ 1

24 ____

____

____ ☐ 3

25 A B C D ☐ 1

26 Translation: ____________________
Nominative singular form: ______________________________________ ☐ 2

27 celerity: ________________________
consensus: ______________________
subversion: _____________________ ☐ 3

28 Imperative verb in Latin: ____________________
Number (singular or plural): ____________________ ☐ 2

29 Relative pronoun in Latin: ____________________
Case: ________________________ ☐ 2

30 A B C ☐ 1

31a Translation: ________________________________ ☐ 1

31b A B C ☐ 1

/50 points for Part A

NOMEN ....

PART B

Understanding the background

Answer all questions on these sheets.
Answer in complete English sentences (unless otherwise instructed).

1 Claudius ______________________ Julius Caesar ______________________

Agricola ______________________ Vespasian ______________________ ☐ 4

2 ____ ☐ 2

3 ____

____

____ ☐ 1

4 ____

____

____ ☐ 2

5 ____

____

____ ☐ 1

6

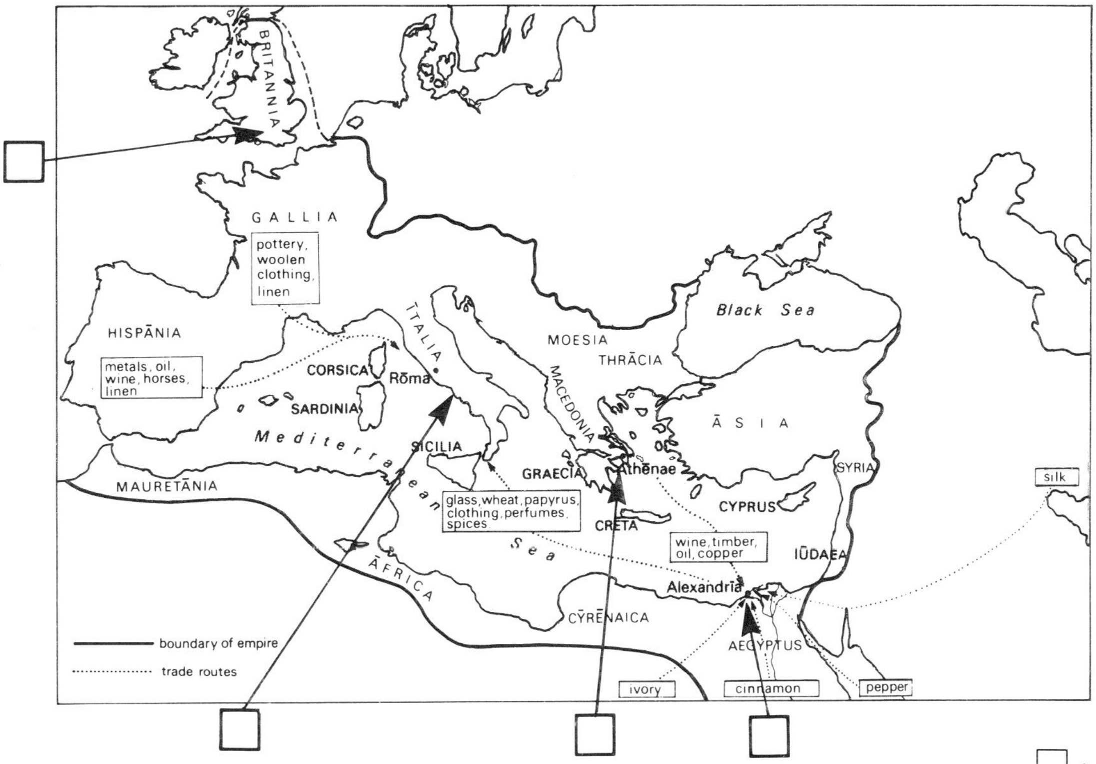

☐ 4

NOMEN ....

7 ______________________________

______________________________ ☐ 1

8 ______________________________

____

______________________________ ☐ 1

9 ______________________________

______________________________ ☐ 1

10 Euclid ______________

Eratosthenes ______________

Hero ______________ ☐ 3

11 ______________________________

______________________________ ☐ 1

12 ______________________________

____

______________________________ ☐ 1

13 ______________________________

______________________________ ☐ 1

14 Latin name: ______________________

Its use: ______________________________

____

______________________________ ☐ 2

/25 points for Part B

/50 + /25 = /75 **points total**

Answer Key

Each question is worth 1 point unless otherwise indicated.

PART A Understanding the story

1a He took him to a part of the city near the Temple of Serapis.

1b Phormio wanted to show Quintus all the shops.

2 Possible answers are: This part of the city was rowdy. This part of the city was dangerous. Few Greeks lived in this part of the city. There were many shopkeepers in this part of the city. (2 points)

3 One could also buy precious gems (silver statues, food) there.

4 They were astonished because an old man pushed Quintus.

5 The old man had pushed Quintus because an amphora, falling from a window, was going to hit Quintus. OR The old man saved Quintus from being hit by a falling amphora, etc.

6 *quam benignus es!*: How kind you are! (2 points)

7 Quintus did not want to talk with Plancus (the man they had seen approaching).

8 Quintus in his anxiety to avoid Plancus did not see the shopkeeper and bumped into him, etc.

9 Quintus was worried (1) because this shopkeeper, who was in a rage (1), was huge and was shouting loudly (vehemently) (1). (3 points total)

10a When the shopkeeper saw Phormio, he (suddenly) smiled/laughed.

10b He smiled because he recognized Phormio / knew Barbillus was Phormio's master / wanted to treat Phormio kindly since his master was very rich / etc.

11 Any one of: The shopkeeper said that Barbillus was very rich. The shopkeeper said that Barbillus bought an expensive gem in the shop the day before.

12 They did not accept the invitation because they did not trust the shopkeeper.

13 which/that/who pleased / was pleasing to everyone/all."

14 Much blood flowed because the cat scratched Quintus' foot.

15 A slave went to get the doctor.

16 Some Alexandrians at this time believed in the power of magic/astrology/superstition / folk remedies in healing of the sick and wounded. (etc.)

17 The doctor also washed the wound.

18 She protected Quintus from the amphora, from the angry shopkeeper, and from being seriously hurt by the cat. (3 points)

19 Quintus said he was fortunate because: the old man saw the amphora; Barbillus (Phormio's master) bought a gem; the doctor lived near the inn. (3 points)

20 C (*neglegens*)

21 A (*vult*)

22 *omnes tabernas* – accusative; *multi tabernarii* – nominative; *gemmas pretiosas* – accusative; *statuas argenteas* – accusative; *pars turbulenta* – nominative; *pars periculosa* – nominative; *pauci Graeci* – nominative (2 points)

23 *urbis*

24 It was difficult for Quintus (1) to walk through the streets (1) because many Alexandrians were blocking his way / blocking him / obstructing him / etc. (1) (3 points total)

25 D (pluperfect)

26 (while) walking; *ambulans* (2 points)

27 celerity *(quam) celerrime* (line 17)
consensus *consensit* (line 18)
subversion *verterunt* (line 19)

28 *venite*; plural (2 points)

29 *quam*; accusative (2 points)

30 B (Your companion didn't intend to push me, did he?)

31a to go

31b B (infinitive)

50 points for Part A

PART B Understanding the background

1 D, B, C, A (4 points)

2 It was built in honor of Neptune and Minerva. (2 points)

3 A client king was a native ruler (usually) who ruled an area or province on behalf of the emperor and was responsible for collecting taxes and/or keeping peace in his area. Such a king had only nominal authority and could not carry on a foreign policy independent of Rome. (Any one correct detail merits 1 point.)

4 Any two details: The general lay-out of the palace was Italianate (Roman). Its mosaics mirrored Roman (Italian) taste. There were stucco friezes / wall paintings / fountains / gardens / marble floors / bronze statues / hypocausts / etc. (2 points)

5 Any one point: The Romans tried to bring peace to tribes that had frequently fought each other in the past. The Romans built roads / temples / fora / houses. The Romans educated the sons of chieftains. Roman rule meant increased trade with the Continent. For some Britons, Roman rule meant increased wealth.

6 Left to right: D, C, A, B (4 points)

7 The lighthouse (Pharos) at Alexandria was one of the Seven Wonders of the Ancient World.

8 The Greeks had achieved their status by being the descendants of the soldiers of Alexander the Great, who had founded the city, and of Ptolemy, to whom Alexander had bequeathed the city.

9 The invention of a method of blowing glass revolutionized the industry.

10 B, A, D (3 points)

11 Any one of several possible answers: They felt they did not need machines since they had many slaves. They might have viewed trade and manufacturing as less dignified than pure research. They may have lacked the technical skills necessary to create industrial machinery.

12 Since the Egyptians had a long history of mummifying bodies, they did not look upon anatomical dissection as distasteful or wicked the way the Greeks did.

13 The Egyptians worshiped Isis for her power to give new life (to people, crops, etc.).

14 Latin: *sistrum* (1 point)
It was used to attract attention and get the people to be quiet (possibly to drown out other evil noises). (1 point)

25 points for Part B
Total: 75 points